39

ERROIS

6/46

MÜLLER THURGAU
16/57

17/59

VALPOLICE
16/54

DOLCETTO
14/46

ERBALU
15/4

SANGIOVESE
16/54

ANC

PRIMI
13/

NERO D'AVOLA

Buvette

Buvette

The Pleasure of Good Food

Jody Williams

with Julia Turshen

Photographs by Gentl & Hyers

Foreword by Mario Batali

GRAND CENTRAL
Life & Style
NEW YORK · BOSTON

Photograph on page ix by Diane Luger. Copyright © 2014 by Hachette Book Group
All other photographs copyright © 2014 by Gentl & Hyers
Foreword copyright © 2014 by Mario Batali

Grand Central Life & Style

Hachette Book Group

1290 Avenue of the Americas

New York, NY 10104

www.GrandCentralLifeandStyle.com

Design by Gary Tooth/Empire Design Studio

Printed in the United States of America

Q-MA

First edition: April 2014

11 10 9 8 7 6 5 4 3

Grand Central Life & Style is an imprint of Grand Central Publishing.
The Grand Central Life & Style name and logo are trademarks of Hachette Book Group, Inc.

The Hachette Speakers Bureau provides a wide range of authors for speaking events. To find out more, go to www.HachetteSpeakersBureau.com or call (866) 376-6591.

The publisher is not responsible for websites (or their content) that are not owned by the publisher.

Library of Congress Cataloging-in-Publication Data
Williams, Jody
  Buvette : the pleasure of good food / Jody Williams with Julia Turshen ;
photographs by Gentl & Hyers. — First edition.
    pages cm
  Includes index.
  ISBN 978-1-4555-2552-2 (hc) — ISBN 978-1-4555-2551-5 (ebook) 1. Cooking, French. 2. Cooking, Italian. 3. Buvette (Restaurant : New York, N.Y.) 4. Gastronomy. I. Turshen, Julia. II. Title.

TX719.W558 2014

641.01'3—dc23

                    2013034360

To all who have encouraged and enjoyed my humble efforts . . .
to those who have shared a memory or a recipe with me in passing . . .
and to those of you who have answered the door and
invited me in.

bu·vette (boo-vet)

[from *boire*, to drink]

Noun: a refreshment stall, café, bar, or pump room;

"How about an apéritif at the buvette down the street?"

Contents

Foreword

I met Jody Williams in the clean, yet dingy and crowded, back of house of the Four Seasons Clift Hotel in San Francisco in 1988. Jody was a banquet porter, decked out in a clean, white lab coat and jeans, and I was a grimy sous-chef in a dishwasher shirt and bib apron. Outside the impressive walls of the 5-star, 5-diamond hotel on Geary and Taylor, was the salty section of the City by the Bay known as the Tenderloin.

There was a revolution going on in San Francisco and Berkeley. "Foodies" had not yet self-monikered, but food had become a thing, and restaurants had become more than a place to eat. They were theatrical settings where politicians and artists and titans of society and industry met to see and be seen, to taste the latest creations of the newly lauded chefs, all decked out in haberdashery and starched chef coats. These chefs were the new heroes—their names: Alice Waters, Jeremiah Tower, Mark Miller, and Wolfgang Puck, among others—and their sparkling creativity collided with the old guard to breed a new kind of restaurant where deliciousness, whimsy, and fun could play together in the previously serious and hallowed halls of fine dining.

Jody and I were hustling greasy shimmering hot boxes filled with banquet plates of Continental food and Queen Mary racks of dirty dishes between elegantly appointed dining rooms and the fluorescent-lit dishwasher room in the unpolished hallways never seen by our wealthy customer base. We would plate banquets for twenty or one hundred people off the sweaty and steamy back line of the kitchen, to be served to the uber-rich, fêting those who would eventually become the Silicon Valley robber barons.

Much has changed.

After meeting and drifting away as coworkers, Jody and I separately went to Italy to travel and cook in small kitchens. We both knew that the truth and the core (as well as the frippery and the pomp) of the California Cuisine revolution was based on the flavors and traditions of Italian and French gastronomy, and each of us had gone on our own journeys to find a piece of that story. Oddly, while I was working in a tiny hill town south of Bologna, I heard about a young American chef working in Reggio Emilia, the swank little town up the Via Emilia, and it turned out to be Jody. We bonded again, loving life in the Emilian Apennines, and then moved on to our new and different paths.

Years later, in New York City, we found each other again when Jody, in cahoots with my at-that-time new friends Joe and Lidia Bastianich, opened a Friulian *frasca* in the theater district called Frico Bar. She worked there and developed some other great restaurants, but I was most excited by Jody pulling the rabbit out of the hat with Buvette, where she and her staff share the love and joy of quality ingredients and dispense wine and coffee and amazing food with a passionate understanding of its unfettered excellence.

West Village locals immediately flocked, and foodies from all over began the pilgrimage to soak up the dreamy simplicity and idiosyncratic design Zen of Jody's quirky and erudite vision, this time through the spectrum of French food and wine.

Needless to say, Jody has achieved a quiet hero status in the New York City gastronomic clique. And while Martha and Alice and Muhlke and the entire pantheon of food aristocracy quietly slide into Buvette daily, there is a certain restraint in the press, as if we are preserving the secret of Buvette's pleasure for an inner circle.

To say that I love Jody and her food and everything about her is understatement, and it is with sweet joy that I see her emerge from the secret circles of foodies into the bright light for all to

discover with this magnificent tome. This cook-book, *Buvette*, captures Jody's pure unadulterated genius. Its supremely poetic design is perceived as simple, but, upon closer inspection, is rich and complex. The elegant and dreamy delicious-ness of the food she creates—understated and nearly literary in its scope—will drive you crazy (in a good way!). The recipes are simple, easy to follow, and carry Jody's well-observed travels and her own remarkable personal story within them.

From the seeds of the food revolution in California in the '80s all the way to the fruits of that movement in 2014, Jody and her food have been evolving, and more and more people come to sit at her table. With the release of *Buvette*, the cookbook, the whole country can partake as she takes center stage. Enjoy!

—*Mario Batali*

Introduction

gas · tro · thèque

I.   Noun: an eating and drinking establishment dedicated to the serious enjoyment of food and wine.

Whenever a guest at Buvette, my *gastrothèque* on a tree-lined street in the West Village, asks me where I learned to cook, I almost always reply jokingly... "I haven't." It isn't entirely true, of course. As a self-taught chef I have learned many things, but as a peripatetic traveler with a great sense of curiosity and adventure I know I am still a student. I will always continue learning how to cook.

The cooking that I love doesn't come from any romanticized view of my upbringing (it was decidedly suburban), or from a rigorous curriculum at a culinary school (I never went), or from formal training anywhere. Rather, it comes from the relationships I have formed with others equally passionate about eating. I have listened to them and have pulled many lessons and recipes from these passing conversations. I remember Alice Waters speaking in awe of a plate of duck confit. The crispness of the skin sounded like a magic trick that I might never be able to perform in my own kitchen. I have been equally inspired by people and places that I have hungrily pursued, fork in hand, throughout my life.

At Buvette, the food and atmosphere have a decidedly Gallic twist. There are fresh eggs and good coffee and warm croissants served with spoonfuls of butter and sweet jam in the morning. Lunch can be a croque-monsieur just out of the oven or a salad of shredded carrots in a bright lemon dressing punctuated with pistachios and coriander. A glass of old-fashioned lemonade with bitters, or a steaming pot of tea with a plate of sugar-dusted madeleines makes for an afternoon respite. In the colder months, a large pot of cassoulet bubbles in the kitchen all night long, and a tarte Tatin waits at the end of the bar. There's always good wine or a smart martini, stirred not shaken. Buvette is about a style of cooking and entertaining that is free from the expected, a comfortable and simple way to enjoy food and drink from sunlight to candlelight.

I love Buvette for its informality and diminutive style. Essentially a bar with thoughtful food, Buvette is free from all the impositions and expectations of a restaurant. It's a neighborhood place, open all day; a place to frequent alone for a quick coffee or a long, lingering supper with friends. Buvette is about reading a newspaper in the morning or having a sparkling rosé on ice late in the afternoon. It is a place where you walk in and seat yourself or add your name in chalk to the waiting list on the edge of the doorframe. At times you may sit so close to your fellow diners that you feel like you're at one table eating together. Everything is visible and anything you might need is within arm's reach. It's about good music and the aroma of warm spiced wine in the winter and crates of blood oranges that are turned into glasses of juice only when you order. It's about orderly stacks of plates and silverware folded into napkins. It's about a convivial staff and blurred boundaries between cook, bartender, and waiter. It's about not doing things in a new way; in fact, it's about very old things, especially things like tradition and comfort. A customer said something to me recently that resonated: Buvette is a lot of a little.

Buvette is a gastrothèque, with a menu full of food that is made simply and served casually (producing superb recipes for home cooks, I might add). As they say, necessity is the mother of invention, and when you're faced with limited space and time, you become inventive. Take oxtails, for example. I adore them, especially in a big bowl served alongside plenty of bread and wine. For something new, I take the braised oxtails off the bone and finish them with bitter chocolate, orange peel, and juniper, a touch of sherry vinegar and honey so the flavor really sings, and then serve them on a thick piece of toast. A big, bold entrée reduced to a single bite, it's bar food that feeds my soul as a chef.

The road to Buvette really began when I was twenty-seven and set out from New York City to learn to cook the old-fashioned way, by knocking on kitchen doors, offering my time and attention in exchange for the chance to learn from other cooks. I did not know it back then, but I would learn to embrace a romantic version of cooking that is steeped in European tradition and culture, where understanding languages and histories is as essential to executing a recipe as knowing how to butcher and bake.

In November 1989, I packed a bag with only a change of clothing, a pair of clogs, a chef's knife, a sharpening steel, an English-Italian dictionary, and a copy of *The Joy of Cooking* (see page 467, How to Skin a Rabbit . . . need I say more?). I spent the next six years in Italy as a cook. On my working documents I was officially listed as an *aiuto-cuoca* level IV, the lowest level of kitchen help there was. Incidentally, I spoke no Italian or French at the time.

I was an apprentice at Caffé Arti e Mestieri in Reggio Emilia, a quaint village divided by the ancient Roman Via Emilia. At Caffé Arti, we tied old tablecloths around our waists for aprons. Like the other cooks, I worked both lunch and dinner with a long break in between. That afternoon break I spent learning to make pasta by hand, or cleaning vegetables that the locals dropped off daily. Before the first guests arrived we would sit down at the table for a family meal. We poured wine into our water and called it *bevanda*. We had meals of broken tortelli or a pumpkin risotto and finished with fresh fruit that we ate with a knife and fork. On Sundays, we gathered at the chef's home for an early supper. He would fry rabbit with rosemary and garlic and serve it on brown paper, accompanied by a salad of sliced fennel and olives—and, of course, many bottles of *vino sfuso*, homemade wine.

Every morning we gathered in the kitchen to make the bread. The pungent yeast filled the air and added to the already aromatic mix of simmering stocks and dried rosemary. This daily baking bestowed tranquility on the kitchen until a shrieking bell announced the arrival of the day's deliveries. In the winter, they delivered wooden crates of local squash, artichokes, radic-chio, and oranges that I stacked in the cellar. During the holidays, sacks of chestnuts and baskets of white truffles arrived at the kitchen door. In summer, crates of tomatoes, still warm from the sun, along with fava beans, melons, and strawberries were procured, and early in the morning we foraged for nettles and arugula. All this food grew within a few miles, close

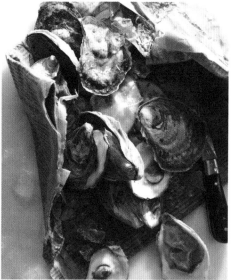

enough for a bicycle ride or a long walk. Cooking and eating locally and seasonally was a way of life. It had a profound impact on how I lived and worked, and still does to this day.

We had no walk-in refrigerators or food processors or industrial mixers at Caffé Arti. I learned how extremely gratifying and sensual it is to cook everything by hand. When you're guided by all your senses, rather than the hum of machines, the food you make maintains more integrity and flavor. Perhaps the most vital lesson I learned at Caffé Arti is that a nurturing environment makes for an excellent cook.

After three years in Reggio I had learned Italian. I moved on to Rome, where I stayed for three more years. I worked all over the Eternal City, including a stint at the famous Hotel Hassler at the top of the Piazza di Spagna, and at Harry's Bar on the Via Veneto, but my favorite job was at a little restaurant with a Michelin star called Da Patrizia e Roberto del Pianeta Terra at Campo de' Fiori.

I knocked on the door and asked, in my American-accented Italian, if they needed a cook, and Chef Roberto Minetti invited me into the kitchen. My culinary education has always benefited from my being within earshot of someone great. Chef Minetti was a grouch, but had wonderful habits like keeping an old wine bottle filled with olive oil and trimmings from truffles and herbs, the stuff that most people throw away. Whenever he poured out some of the oil to dress a salad, he would simply add more to the bottle and give it a shake. His ricotta cake, a recipe from the 1600s, was so dense with spices it looked like pumpkin pie.

Campo de' Fiori is the oldest market in Rome and was literally at our doorstep. All our vegetables and fish came from the market—squash blossoms, scampi, swordfish, *misticanza*, puntarella, *ovuli*, and porcini mushrooms. The *guanciale*, cured pork jowls, for our bucatini came from

the acclaimed Antica Norcineria Viola. Believe me, I knew how lucky I was.

After six years in Italy, I had a chance to work in Japan for a few months. Even in a place where I can't speak or read the language, I've always been able to follow along in the kitchen since so much of what there is to learn is purely visual. At times, communication can be very silent, and I'm quite comfortable with silence. As it happens, the Japanese love French food and especially French wine. I picked up so much knowledge in Japan: specifically, attention to detail, the importance of presentation, and even how to fry properly.

Returning to New York, I brought back everything I had soaked up in my years of living abroad. Cooking in restaurants in New York City in the late 1980s and early '90s was like working in the Wild West. Cooking was accessible work that attracted all sorts of characters, and restaurants were places where not only could you start at the bottom and move your way up, you *had* to start at the bottom. Now, the industry is more regulated, accountable, and well behaved, but it still offers great opportunities to learn, as long as you have an appetite for the work.

At a certain point, I had the courage and support to go out on my own; I felt ready to use all my experiences, all the objects and recipes I had collected. In 2010, I opened Buvette.

Assembling this book has been an opportunity to reflect on the inspirations I've had in so many different kitchens around the world with so many people. Turning this all into food that can easily be made and served at home was a refreshingly easy translation as all of my cooking is simple, handmade, and straightforward. Buvette is more than a place; it's also a feeling and an idea. It's a way to cook, entertain, and live. It's a recipe for living more meaningfully.

—Jody

Notes Before You Start

INGREDIENTS

DAIRY AND EGGS

All dairy and eggs are organic.

All butter is unsalted.

Cultured butter (butter made with fermented cream) is unsalted and seasoned with Maldon sea salt as it is served.

All eggs are large and free range.

All milk is always whole milk.

All cream is heavy cream, which is sometimes labeled whipping cream.

If you can't find crème fraîche, make it (page 258).

OLIVE OIL

Plentiful extra-virgin olive oil is essential. I use it as much at breakfast and brunch on eggs and toast as I do at lunch and dinner. Richard Olney once said, "Olive oil is the best sauce," and I think that is really true.

MEATS, POULTRY, GAME, SHELLFISH, AND FISH

All should be as high quality as possible, whether that means grass-fed beef, antibiotic-free poultry, or wild, fresh fish.

PRODUCE

Produce is seasonal, local, organic, and ready to eat. This means **ripeness** is important. If we are serving a plate of persimmons with cheese, or adding figs and prosciutto to *schiacciata,* or planning to lunch on tomatoes, ripeness will trump any tricks a chef might have.

Produce must be thoroughly washed and dried. To wash produce properly, start with tepid water, and finish washing it with cold water to freshen it.

FRESHNESS

How can it be described as fresh if it has a cap on it and is refrigerated? It boggles my mind to see how often the word *fresh* is abused. Fresh is unaltered, never processed. For example, if a recipe calls for "freshly squeezed lemon juice," I will squeeze the lemon immediately before adding it to whatever dish I am creating, not in advance.

WATER

While a good chicken broth is both a marvel to master and enjoy, I often prefer to use water instead of stocks. Water is an overlooked and underused ingredient. Water is purifying and doesn't distract or muddle flavors. It requires the best ingredients because they have nothing to hide behind. Water will elongate flavors as well as balance them, as in the case of pickling.

PANTRY AND BAKING

All spices are freshly ground, either in a spice mill or by hand in a mortar and pestle.

When coarse salt is called for it is at minimum kosher salt and at best a good sea salt such as Maldon or sel gris de Guérande.

All flour is unbleached all-purpose white flour unless otherwise specified (i.e., buckwheat or whole wheat flour).

All yeast is active dry yeast, also sometimes labeled "rapid rise."

All sugar is granulated white sugar unless otherwise specified (e.g., superfine or powdered sugar).

SOURCES

There are no processed ingredients in any of my recipes. At Buvette, I don't even offer artificial sweeteners or decaf coffee. This is not just because I don't have space for them but also because I like the idea of having the real thing or nothing—and not anything in between.

Italian ingredients such as good olive oil, rice for risotto, and sun-dried tomatoes can be found in specialty shops or at buonitalia.com or eataly.com.

Special French meats, and ingredients like duck confit and duck fat, can be found at dartagnan.com, and other specialty French ingredients can usually be found at deananddeluca.com.

All my cheese comes from Anne Saxelby, who has a shop, Saxelby Cheesemongers, in the Essex Street Market in New York. Find the best cheese shop near you, then become friends and ask questions. The same goes for your fish store, bakery, wine shop, and produce stand.

Honey and maple syrups come from Catskill Provisions (catskillprovisions.com).

TOOLS AND EQUIPMENT

WITH A SPOON AND FORK . . .

I have a collection of vintage rolling pins, spring whisks, measuring cups, and hand juicers. I also have the *de rigueur batterie de cuisine* (all the essential equipment and tools) for a chef. This trove is functional and inspiring, but I prefer to use just a few things: my Japanese chef's knife, a tablespoon, and a fork. I will grate a block of pecorino Romano cheese over a salad with the tines of a fork before I find my grater,

and I prefer to fillet a fish just out of the oven with the back of my spoon rather than reach for a spatula. I'm a bit of an old soul, more at home with turn-of-the-century technique and kitchen sense. Sometimes when I am coaching my cooks, I will ask them, "How would your grandmother make this dish?"

PART 1.

MORNINGS

Mornings

Breakfast is easy to love. More than any other meal, it can embrace both sweet and savory; it can be quick and light, or quite substantial. And, if you'd like to prolong this special meal, you can linger while you finish one more cup of coffee. Breakfast also has more specificity to it than any other meal. How you take your coffee is so particular. Or maybe it's how long you steep your tea, how soft you like your egg yolk, how crisp your bacon. Bread can be sliced thick or thin, toasted, cut in half or in triangles. All these decisions are not just preferences, but a collection of small rituals that define you.

The following recipes are great for those mornings when you sleep late, or you want to make a weekday special. They are also great for a *nuit blanche*, because after a long night of fun sometimes breakfast can be your last meal of the day. No matter when you prepare these dishes, take care with the small things too—wrap your warm toast in a cloth napkin, squeeze your own juice, decant your jam into a beautiful little bowl.
Your intention really does count.

A FEW MORNING MENUS

BREAKFAST IN BED

Omelette

Toast with Orange and Campari Marmalade

Freshly Squeezed Orange Juice

A BRUNCH GATHERING

Toasted Oatmeal

Eggs en Cocotte

Yogurt Parfaits with Maple Nuts

Summer Fruit Salad

Whole Wheat Scones with Currants

Carrot Spoon Breads

Classic 1930 Bloody Marys and Green Tomato Bloody Marys

UN PETIT DÉJEUNER

Crêpes with Nutella

Bomboloni

Chocolat Chaud

Oeufs Brouillés

Brouillade is how the French describe perfectly cooked scrambled eggs. At Buvette, we make them using the milk steamer on our espresso machine. It is not only quick and efficient but it also adds to the charm of having your breakfast made in front of you, literally at arm's length, gastrothèque style. At home, you can successfully achieve the same incredibly creamy, nearly custardlike texture using a small, heavy saucepan on the stovetop.

[SERVES 1; EASILY MULTIPLIED]

3 large eggs

2 tablespoons good-quality
unsalted butter

Coarse salt

Freshly ground black pepper

Crack the eggs into a bowl and vigorously whisk together.

Meanwhile, set a small, heavy saucepan over medium heat and add half of the butter. Once the butter has melted, add the whisked eggs. Using a wooden spoon, stir the eggs constantly while they cook, being sure to get all of the bits off of the sides of the pot (not unlike you do when you're making a risotto). Do not turn the heat up—you want the eggs to cook gently and lovingly and not take on any color.

You are looking for a mixture that's cooked through, but still loose enough to pour. To get to that perfect moment, pull the pot off the heat when the eggs begin to form small curds. Another good indicator of this moment is when the bottom of the pot will hold the lines your wooden spoon makes as you draw it through the eggs. At that precise moment when the eggs are *just* cooked, remove the pot from the heat and stir in the remaining 1 tablespoon butter (the pot will hold more than enough residual heat to melt the butter into the eggs).

Serve immediately with a sprinkle of salt and a few grinds of pepper. While these are heaven on their buttery own, welcome embellishments include a spoonful of crème fraîche or caviar, or both, and a sprinkle of fried shallots with a few shavings of bottarga (dried tuna roe). Slices of prosciutto or smoked salmon draped over the eggs are very nice too. Be sure to add some large caperberries and crème fraîche to the plate if you go down the smoked salmon route. With any of these variations, an accompanying stack of toast goes without saying, buttered or drenched in olive oil of course. »CONTINUES

RECIPE NOTES

1. To get the creamiest, richest scrambled eggs, it's vital that the eggs are mixed well. Like a proper cocktail, there should be a little froth on top.

2. I mix the eggs with what some people call a spring whisk. The coiled spring agitates the eggs more than a traditional whisk, ensuring that they are incredibly well incorporated.

3. It's important to use a small, heavy saucepan to make these since the large surface area of a skillet supplies too much direct heat to the eggs. You never want your brouillade to brown or cook too quickly—the small size of a saucepan helps you control the heat and keep them blissfully creamy.

4. Please substitute olive oil for butter as you wish.

On Fresh Orange Juice

It is important to understand that "fresh" is nothing other than immediate. And if there's an option to do something by hand, that's how we do it. Not only does this inform the type of food we prepare and the feeling it evokes, it also cuts down on how much noise we make! This is especially true when it comes to the fresh orange juice that we squeeze—to order, manually, in an old press. And while there's nothing wrong with using standard juice oranges, if you can find a variety of citrus fruits it's nice to make combinations, like blood orange and tangerine, or grapefruit and Meyer lemon. If your juice is very tart, you can serve it alongside a shaker of sugar, like they do in Italy. Of course any and all citrus juice is also great with a bit of Champagne!

Duck Eggs with Brown Butter and Sage

Duck eggs cooked in browned butter and sage is simple food. Of course you can prepare regular chicken eggs this way, but I appreciate the rich taste of duck eggs and the nutty flavor of brown butter.

[MAKES 3 EGGS; EASILY MULTIPLIED]

2 tablespoons unsalted butter

4 fresh sage leaves

3 duck eggs

Coarse salt

Freshly ground black pepper

Preheat the oven to 400°F.

Place the butter in a medium skillet over medium-high heat. Add the sage leaves and cook, stirring occasionally, until the butter turns brown. Gently crack the eggs into the pan and place it in the oven (alternatively, you can turn the heat to low and cover the pan with a lid). Bake until the egg whites are just set and the yolks retain a bright yellow color, about 5 minutes. Serve immediately, sprinkled with salt and pepper. Don't forget about the browned butter left in the pan. Be sure to pour it over the eggs when serving.

Ramps and Eggs

Ramps, small wild onions with dark green leaves and pale red roots, arrive early during springtime on the East Coast and disappear quickly. Both their ephemeral presence and strong flavor make them a real treat. I like to prepare them as simply as possible by wilting them in olive oil and combining them with eggs.

[SERVES 1 GENEROUSLY]

3 tablespoons extra-virgin olive oil

1 small bunch ramps, root ends trimmed and discarded, thoroughly washed

Coarse salt

3 large eggs

Preheat the oven to 400°F.

Warm the olive oil in a medium skillet over medium-high heat. Add the ramps and a large pinch of salt. Cook, stirring occasionally, until the ramps just begin to soften, about 5 minutes.

Gently crack the eggs into the pan directly alongside the ramps and place the pan in the oven (alternatively, you can reduce the heat to low and cover the pan with a lid). Bake until the egg whites are just set and the yolk retains a bright yellow color, about 5 minutes. Serve immediately, sprinkled with additional salt.

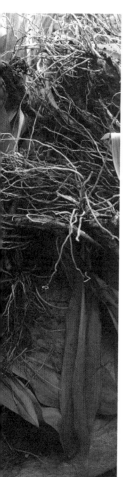

Poached Eggs over Scafata

In Italian, *scafata* means "shelled beans," but when you order it, it often includes a mix of vegetables. I always make scafata with fresh fava beans, springtime's gift to the kitchen. (See the recipe introduction on page 83 for instructions on shelling favas.) Feel free to include asparagus or fresh lima beans. Note that this dish is welcome anytime of the day and makes for a great lunch, especially with a glass of rosé from Provence.

[SERVES 4]

½ cup extra-virgin olive oil, plus more for serving

3 garlic cloves, peeled and minced

2 dried red chilies, or a large pinch of red chili flakes

4 baby artichokes, trimmed and cut into eighths

1 cup peeled fava beans

½ cup fresh shelled peas

2 scallions, white and light green parts only, thinly sliced

½ bunch escarole, roughly chopped

Leaves from 2 sprigs fresh basil

Leaves from 2 sprigs fresh mint

Coarse salt

2 tablespoons white wine vinegar

4 large eggs

Shaved pecorino Romano cheese, for serving

Combine the olive oil, garlic, chilies, and artichokes in a medium saucepan over medium heat. Bring to a boil and cook, partially covered, until the artichoke pieces are just beginning to get tender, about 5 minutes.

Add the fava beans, peas, and scallions and cook until the beans are just tender, about 2 minutes. Add the escarole, basil, and mint and let the mixture simmer until the artichokes are completely tender, 3 to 5 minutes more. Season to taste with salt, then divide the scafata evenly among four shallow bowls.

Meanwhile bring 3 inches of water and the vinegar to a boil in a large saucepan. Lower the heat so that the water is just gently simmering. Crack each egg into a small ramekin and carefully slip each one into the simmering water, spacing them so that their whites do not touch. Cook the eggs until the whites are just set, 3 to 4 minutes. Using a slotted spoon, carefully remove the eggs from the water and transfer them immediately to the plated scafata. Top each poached egg with a few shavings of pecorino Romano and a drizzle of olive oil. Serve immediately.

Omelette

The choices for omelettes are limited only by your imagination. All you need is a nice salad of fresh greens and radishes dressed simply with oil, salt, and a few drops of vinegar served alongside, and a glass of wine.

[MAKES 1 OMELETTE]

2 large eggs

Coarse salt

3 tablespoons chopped mixed leafy herbs
(I like a mix of chives, chervil, and tarragon,
but use whatever you like and is fresh)

1 tablespoon unsalted butter

Freshly ground black pepper

Preheat the oven to 400°F.

Crack the eggs into a bowl and add a large pinch of salt. Vigorously whisk together and stir in two-thirds of the herb mixture. Set the egg mixture aside.

In a small, 6-inch diameter sauté pan set over medium heat, melt the butter. (If your pan is not well seasoned you may need more butter.)

As the butter melts, tilt the pan to make sure the butter evenly coats the pan. Pour in the whisked eggs and continue cooking over medium heat until the eggs begin to set, but are not cooked through, roughly 3 minutes, keeping in mind that the eggs will continue cooking off the heat. This is the point where you can add Parmigiano-Reggiano and butter, ham and Gruyère, or goat cheese and leeks if you wish. A good omelette will have a creamy texture and remain bright yellow.

Season with salt and pepper, and then begin to fold the omelette.

To remove the omelette, tilt the pan toward the serving plate and gently free it with a spatula until it slides halfway onto the plate. Now fold it over onto itself to form a half-moon. Serve sprinkled with the remaining 1 tablespoon herbs and an additional pinch of salt.

> **RECIPE NOTE**
> If you are making omelettes for more than one, I suggest using your oven as I do at Buvette. It is a fast and easy way to make a beautiful omelette. Begin by melting the butter in a small pan on the stovetop as above, but when you add the eggs, transfer the pan to a 400°F oven to continue cooking, about 5 minutes. If you wish to fill your omelette with spinach or leeks, etc., do so as soon as it sets and then return it to the oven to finish cooking. Remove and follow the instructions for plating above.

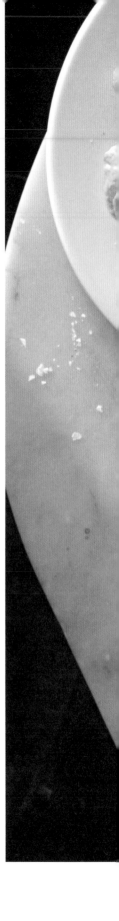

A Well-Seasoned Pan

If you have a favorite omelette pan, I am sure, in time, it will become an heirloom. The more you use it, the more it will take on a natural patina, and its surface will become increasingly immune to sticking.

Mornings   15

Oeufs à la Coque with Savory Toasts

Oeufs à la Coque, a classic breakfast of soft-boiled eggs, served with thin *bâtons* of toast (sometimes referred to in English as "soldiers") is so simple, yet also feels so special. To make a slightly elevated version, I flavor the toasts with Parmigiano-Reggiano cheese and thyme and wrap them in prosciutto. The toasts also make great snacks to have with cocktails.

[SERVES 4]

4 slices country bread

2 tablespoons extra-virgin olive oil

Small handful grated
Parmigiano-Reggiano cheese

Leaves from 2 sprigs fresh thyme

8 slices prosciutto, cut in half lengthwise

8 large eggs

Coarse salt

Freshly ground black pepper

Preheat the oven to 400°F.

Cut each slice of bread into 4 long bâtons (each should be about the size of your index finger). Place the bâtons on a baking sheet in an even layer and bake in the oven, turning the bread every so often, until dry and golden brown, 5 to 10 minutes.

Remove the baking sheet from the oven, and drizzle the oil evenly over the toasts. Scatter over the grated Parmigiano-Reggiano and the thyme leaves so that each toast is hit with a bit of both. Wrap each toast with a strip of the prosciutto and then place the toasts back on the baking sheet, being sure to leave a bit of space between them.

Return the baking sheet to the oven and bake the toasts until the prosciutto is just barely beginning to crisp, 5 to 10 minutes.

Meanwhile, boil a pot of water. Gently add the eggs to the water and cook for exactly 3 minutes. Using a slotted spoon, transfer the eggs to bowls or individual egg cups if you have them. Serve the eggs with the toasts.

To eat, use a table knife to cut the top off of each egg, and use a little spoon to dig out the beautifully cooked egg, spreading the yolk on your savory toast, or even dipping your toast into the egg yolk. However you please, really.

Buvette / The Pleasure of Good Food

Uova Sode
with Seasoned Salt

This idea was inspired by the Italian Easter tradition of wrapping chocolate eggs in colorful paper with a surprise inside. I use a vintage wire egg basket for holding hard-boiled eggs that are wrapped in brown paper. To make hard-boiled eggs less ordinary, a pinch of seasoned salt goes into the center of a square of parchment paper, and the egg is placed on the parchment with the seasoned salt. When it's all wrapped up, the egg and seasoned salt become a portable snack that can be put in your pocket and enjoyed anytime hunger strikes.

[MAKES AS MANY EGGS AS YOU LIKE]

Eggs
Seasoned Salt (page 268)

Place the eggs in a small saucepan and cover with cold water. Set the pot over high heat and bring the water to a boil. Cook the eggs for 2 minutes, turn off the heat, and cover the pot. Let the pot sit for 5 minutes, then drain off the water and let the eggs sit until they're cool enough to handle. Wrap the eggs with a pinch of the seasoned salt in parchment paper as described above, if you'd like. When you're ready to feel like you are out on a picnic, unwrap the parchment, spread it out like a little place mat, peel the egg, and dip it into the salt as you eat. When you're finished, you can wrap up the shell in the paper and toss it in the trash—easy cleanup!

> **Knowing Good Eggs**
> *I use a lot of chicken eggs, especially during brunch on Saturdays and Sundays. At Buvette, we go through 150 dozen—that's 1,800—every weekend. That said, I think we know good eggs. When shopping for eggs, look for purveyors at your local farmers' market who are raising chickens sustainably. They might cost a bit more than the ones at the supermarket, but fresh, organic eggs are not only preferable for the environment, they taste significantly better too.*

Fritatta with Zucchini and Squash Blossoms

A frittata can be served warm or at room temperature with or without a salad. Zucchini and squash blossoms are some of my favorites, but feel free to use whatever is in season, or even leftovers like ham or cheese you may have on hand. Leftover fritatta can be made into a panini—my favorite way to enjoy it, really.

[SERVES 4]

1 small zucchini, ends trimmed off and discarded

6 squash blossoms

Extra-virgin olive oil

Coarse salt

8 large eggs, beaten together

6 fresh basil leaves, roughly torn

Freshly ground black pepper

Small handful grated pecorino Romano cheese

Grilled bread, for serving

Preheat the oven to 400°F.

Using a mandoline or a sharp knife, thinly slice the zucchini into rounds and set it aside.

Using your hands, remove and discard the stems from the squash blossoms, tear the blossoms into big pieces, and set them aside.

Heat 3 tablespoons of olive oil in a skillet over medium-high heat. Add the zucchini and cook, stirring occasionally, until softened and a tiny bit brown, 5 minutes. Season the zucchini with a pinch of salt. Turn off the heat, pour the eggs over the squash, then drizzle the eggs with an additional tablespoon or two of olive oil. Evenly lay the torn squash blossoms over the eggs and place the skillet into the oven.

Bake until the eggs are just set, about 10 minutes. Immediately remove the frittata from the oven and give it one final drizzle of olive oil, a grind of freshly cracked pepper, and a sprinkle of the grated cheese, and scatter over the torn basil. Cut the frittata into wedges and serve with grilled bread drizzled with olive oil.

Uova al Forno

Amatriciana is a popular pasta sauce often made with guanciale, or cured pork jowls, and onions, tomatoes, and chilies. This Roman specialty is equally delicious as the sauce in *uova al forno,* or baked eggs.

[SERVES 4]

One 28-ounce can whole peeled tomatoes with their juices

2 tablespoons extra-virgin olive oil

1 dried red chili or pinch red chili flakes

1 garlic clove, peeled and minced

1½ teaspoons coarse salt

½ pound smoked bacon, cut into 1-inch-thick lardons

1 large yellow onion, peeled and thickly sliced

4 to 8 large eggs

Grated pecorino Romano cheese, for serving

Preheat the oven to 400°F.

Place the entire contents of the can of tomatoes into a bowl and crush by hand. Set aside.

In a medium saucepan, warm the olive oil over medium heat, add the chili and the garlic, and sauté for 30 seconds. Add the crushed tomatoes and salt and bring the mixture to a boil. Reduce the heat and let simmer for 30 minutes, or until slightly thickened.

Meanwhile, cook the bacon in a large skillet over high heat for 2 or 3 minutes until the fat has rendered. Add the onions and reduce the heat to medium. Cook, stirring occasionally, until the onions are soft and a little bit brown and the bacon is a tiny bit crisp, about 20 minutes. Transfer the tomato sauce to the bacon and onion mixture and stir to combine.

At this point you can leave the sauce in the pan and bake the eggs directly in the pan, or divide the sauce evenly among four individual baking dishes, being sure to evenly distribute the bacon and onions among the dishes. Whether you're working in one big skillet or in four individual baking dishes, use a wooden spoon to make indentations in the sauce, and crack the eggs into the indentations. Use 1 or 2 eggs per person depending on how hungry you and your friends are.

Transfer the skillet or dishes to the oven and bake until the eggs are just set, about 12 minutes.

Serve immediately, with plenty of the grated cheese on top.

Asparagus Milanese

You have to leave the window open, so to speak, to be creative when you cook, as so many recipes emerge from problems (e.g., lemonade from too many lemons). I find the best dishes happen when you have embellished something left over, or have replaced a missing ingredient, or from any time when you've treated a challenge like an opportunity. This elegant dish can also make use of an abundance of leftover asparagus.

[SERVES 2]

Coarse salt

A small handful of asparagus, tough ends removed and discarded

2 tablespoons unsalted butter

2 good-quality large eggs

Freshly ground black pepper

A little finely grated Parmigiano-Reggiano cheese

Bring a small pot of water to a boil over high heat and season with salt. Add the asparagus and cook until just tender, about 2 minutes. Drain immediately and transfer to paper towels and let dry off for a minute or so.

Heat the butter in a small skillet over medium heat. Add the asparagus to the butter and get the spears together in the center of the pan. Crack the eggs directly on top of the asparagus and sprinkle the tops with a pinch of salt. Cover the pan with a lid (or another skillet, inverted). Cook until the egg whites are just set, about 2 minutes. Uncover the pan, slide a spatula under the asparagus, and transfer to a warm plate, being careful to keep the eggs intact. Spoon the butter that's accumulated in the bottom of the pan over the asparagus and the eggs and sprinkle the whole thing with a final pinch of salt and a few healthy grinds of black pepper.

Serve immediately with a little bit of Parmigiano-Reggiano on top, because *why not*?

Piperade

Piperade, a traditional Southwestern French dish of sweet bell peppers and pork, is made here with spicy chorizo. The combination evokes the flavors of sausage with peppers and onions, the Italian-American carnival classic. Topped with eggs, this makes a savory, satisfying meal that's especially beneficial for curing brutal hangovers. Note that if you can't find fresh chorizo, you can finely chop dried chorizo.

[SERVES 4]

3 tablespoons extra-virgin olive oil	2 bell peppers (whatever color you'd like), stemmed, seeded, and sliced	3 garlic cloves, peeled and minced
½ pound fresh chorizo, meat removed from casings (casings discarded) or ½ pound finely chopped dried chorizo	1 small yellow onion, peeled and sliced	Coarse salt
		8 large eggs
		Toast, for serving

Preheat the oven to 400°F.

Heat the olive oil in a large skillet set over medium-high heat. Crumble in the chorizo and cook, stirring occasionally, until the meat is browned and starting to get a little bit crisp, about 10 minutes.

Add all of the vegetables and cook, stirring occasionally, until the vegetables are soft and browned (color is flavor!) and the whole thing smells intoxicating, about 20 minutes. Season the mixture to taste with salt and set it aside.

At this point you can leave the vegetable mixture in the pan and bake the eggs directly in the pan, or divide the mixture evenly among four individual baking dishes. Whether you're working in one big skillet or in four individual baking dishes, use a wooden spoon to make indentations in the sauce, and crack the eggs into the indentations.

Transfer the skillet or dishes to the oven and bake until the eggs are just set, about 12 minutes.

Serve immediately.

RECIPE NOTES

Without the chorizo, this recipe works well as a vegetarian option. You can also substitute soaked and chopped salt cod for the sausage.

Instead of baking the eggs, you can scramble them and fold them into the vegetable mixture or serve them alongside the vegetable mixture.

On Toast and Its Toppings

I like toast with butter and I really like it with olive oil. When I season a piece of toast with olive oil, I season it almost like a steak. I give it a good pour and, with a generous hand, sprinkle it with sea salt and black pepper. It's a savory, crunchy vehicle for nearly everything good in life. I serve stacks of toast with a crock of duck rillettes (see page 140), or soft Oeufs Brouillés (page 5), and even a good piece of cheese.

Crêpes

Walking down the street in Paris, eating a huge crêpe with lemon, butter, and sugar, is a fond food memory evocative of what the French call *sur le pouce*, "on the thumb," the feeling of having something good in hand. In addition to being so wonderfully nostalgic, the really astounding thing about a crêpe is its versatility (see variations below). Note that the batter must rest for a few hours, so plan ahead.

[MAKES A GENEROUS PINT OF BATTER; ABOUT A DOZEN 8-INCH CRÊPES]

¾ cup unbleached all-purpose flour

Pinch coarse salt

2 large eggs

4 tablespoons (½ stick) unsalted butter, melted and cooled, plus more for cooking the crêpes

1¼ cups whole milk

In a large mixing bowl, whisk together the flour, salt, and eggs to make a paste. Whisk in the butter. Slowly whisk in the milk, being sure to take your time so that you avoid lumps. Cover the bowl with plastic wrap, or transfer the batter to an airtight container and refrigerate for at least 4 hours or up to 3 days before cooking (see Recipe Note, page 30).

Once the batter has rested, heat up a slick of butter in a small skillet, preferably nonstick (if not, just use more butter!) over medium heat. Pour in just a little less than ¼ cup of batter. Tilt the pan in a circular motion so that the batter finds itself in an even layer on the bottom of the pan. Cook the crêpe until the bottom is just golden brown, about 1½ minutes, loosen the edges with a spatula, and turn the crêpe. Cook until it's nicely browned on the opposite side, about 1 minute more. Transfer the crêpe to a warm plate and fill it or garnish it however you'd like (some of my favorites are listed on pages 30–31). Repeat the process until you've used up all of the batter. »CONTINUES

RECIPE NOTES
The Versatility of Crêpes

Crêpes can be a snack or a whole meal. They can be sweet or savory. They can be made ahead and folded with elegant fillings like good ham and Gruyère cheese and baked later on. You can make small crêpes, stack them up, and serve them alongside jars of Nutella and jam, turning any morning or afternoon after school into a kid-friendly project. You can make a big floppy sombrero of a crêpe, place it in a large bowl, grate chocolate or scatter berries over the top, and serve it to guests who can fold it up however they'd like. Crêpes can be used like sheets of pasta and baked with layers of cheese and vegetables; they can be julienned, caramelized, and tossed with warm apples and cinnamon. Even a botched crêpe can be stirred in the pan with a spoon and served in a bowl with butter and sugar to be thoroughly enjoyed.

Resting Your Crêpe Better

Rested batter is better batter. When you make your batter in advance and let it rest before using it, it means that the proteins activated by combining liquid with the gluten in flour will calm down. This is a good thing as it makes for a more relaxed mixture, a more cooperative mixture, a batter that's easier to work with, and ultimately, a more beautiful crêpe.

BRETON GALETTE / BUCKWHEAT CRÊPE

Prepare the Crêpes as directed, but substitute ¼ cup buckwheat flour for ¼ cup of the unbleached all-purpose flour. Fill each crêpe with a slice of good ham (prosciutto cotto if you can find it), a small handful of grated Gruyère, or a slice of Brie or other soft cheese (Époisses is really lovely here), and a sage leaf and fold the crêpe into quarters. Transfer the filled crêpes to a buttered baking dish and bake in a 400°F oven until crisp and golden brown, about 10 minutes. These can also happily get a sunny-side-up egg tucked inside as well.

CHESTNUT CRÊPES

For chestnut crêpes, use the Crêpes recipe, but substitute 3 tablespoons chestnut flour for 3 tablespoons of the unbleached all-purpose flour.

CRÊPES WITH LEMON, BUTTER, AND SUGAR

Make Crêpes. Spread each warm crêpe with a slick of good butter, sprinkle over a bit of granulated sugar, and squeeze over a few drops of fresh lemon juice. Roll the crêpe and eat immediately while warm, dusted with powdered sugar, if you'd like.

CRÊPES WITH NUTELLA

Make Crêpes. Spread each crêpe with a heaping tablespoon of Nutella, then fold into a triangle. Place the stuffed crêpes in a baking dish, dot with butter, and bake at 400°F until crisp and golden brown, about 10 minutes. Serve dusted with powdered sugar.

CRÊPE RIBBONS WITH APPLES, WALNUTS, AND CINNAMON

For each serving, julienne half an apple and toss it in a pan with 2 tablespoons of melted butter, a small handful of chopped walnuts, a pinch of salt, a spoonful of sugar, and a pinch of ground cinnamon. Cook until the apples are just beginning to soften, about 5 minutes. Meanwhile, roll 3 crêpes (made from Crêpes recipe) like a cigar and cut crosswise into ribbons (they should look like fettuccine). Add the sliced crêpes to the apples, stir to combine, and then let the mixture cook until the bottom is crisp and browned, about 5 minutes. Serve immediately in a bowl like pasta, and say good-bye to cold cereal forever.

Brioche à Tête and Bomboloni

Decadent bread enriched with butter, milk, and eggs, brioche is a staple in French kitchens. I primarily use the dough for *brioche à tête,* little brioche rolls made in fluted molds that go by the same name, and also *bomboloni,* amazingly delicious, not-too-sweet doughnuts.

[MAKES A DOZEN SMALL BRIOCHES À TÊTE
OR A BAKER'S DOZEN (13) BOMBOLONI]

½ cup plus 1 tablespoon whole milk

1 large egg

1 large egg yolk

2½ cups unbleached all-purpose flour, plus extra for dusting

¼ cup sugar

¾ teaspoon coarse salt

¾ teaspoon active dry yeast

5 tablespoons (½ stick plus 1 tablespoon) unsalted butter, at room temperature, plus more for greasing

IF YOU'RE MAKING BRIOCHE À TÊTE, YOU WILL ALSO NEED:

An extra beaten egg, for brushing the tops

Extra sugar, for dusting

Butter and jam, for serving

IF YOU'RE MAKING BOMBOLONI, YOU WILL ALSO NEED:

Oil, for frying (corn, peanut, vegetable, canola, or grapeseed oil all work well)

Extra sugar, preferably superfine sugar,* for rolling

In a small bowl, whisk together the milk, egg, and egg yolk.

Meanwhile, combine the flour, sugar, salt, and yeast in the bowl of a stand mixer fitted with a dough hook and mix briefly just to combine. Add the egg mixture to the dry ingredients and set the mixer on high speed. Let the dough mix until it goes from quite loose to the consistency of very thick cake batter, 2 to 3 minutes. Don't panic while it's mixing in fear that it won't thicken and think you need to add more flour—just let it keep mixing and it will get there on its own. Once it's thickened, stop the machine and scrape down the sides and the bottom of the bowl with a rubber spatula to make sure there are no pockets of flour or egg hiding anywhere.

Turn the mixer to medium speed and add the butter a little bit at a time (approximately 1 tablespoon per addition). Once all of the butter has been ≫CONTINUES

* While you can roll the bomboloni in regular granulated sugar and they will be nothing less than perfect, superfine sugar will create a coating that looks almost like frosty snow, which is not required but is quite beautiful.

added, let the dough mix until it begins to pull away from the sides of the bowl and starts to gather on the dough hook, about 5 minutes.

Butter the surface of a large mixing bowl, and transfer the dough to the bowl, making sure to use your fingers or a rubber spatula. Using your fingertips, spread the surface of the dough with a tiny bit more butter, and cover the bowl with plastic wrap. Set the dough aside until it has risen a little bit and is quite soft to the touch, either a couple of hours at room temperature, or overnight in the refrigerator. Know that brioche, heavy with all of its rich dairy, is a slow riser. Don't be disheartened if the dough hasn't doubled in size like most bread doughs. It will be just fine.

Once the dough has relaxed and risen, generously flour your work surface. Break off walnut-size pieces of dough (about 1.5 ounces each) and roll them on the work surface with the palm of your hand to form even balls. You should have 13 pieces.

To make brioche à tête, thoroughly butter and flour a dozen small, 1½-inch diameter brioche à tête molds.* Transfer 12 of the dough balls to each of the prepared molds. Using the tip of your index finger, indent the top of each brioche à tête. Break the thirteenth dough ball into a dozen small pieces and roll them to form little balls. Place one small ball into each indentation.

Drape the formed brioche with a clean kitchen towel and let them have their second and final rise for an hour or two at room temperature. You're looking for dough that maybe hasn't quite doubled in size, but has risen a little and taken on some new air, and, most important, appears relaxed.

Meanwhile, preheat the oven to 350°F.

Using a pastry brush or your fingertips, brush the top of each brioche à tête with some of the extra beaten egg. At this point you can sprinkle the top with coarse sugar if you'd like. Place the brioche in the oven and bake until beautifully browned, about 20 minutes.

Let the brioche cool on a wire rack and enjoy just slightly warm or at room temperature with plenty of butter and jam alongside.

To make bomboloni, transfer the 13 dough balls to a floured baking sheet and cover with a clean kitchen towel for an hour or two. You're looking for dough that hasn't quite doubled in size, but has risen a little and taken on some new air, and, most important, appears relaxed.

Meanwhile, heat 2 inches of oil in a large, heavy pot set over medium-high heat until it reaches 375°F, or until a pinch of flour sizzles on contact. Dust the excess flour from the bomboloni and carefully place them, in batches if necessary depending on the size of your pot, in the hot oil. Fry, turning occasionally, until browned on all sides, about 5 minutes total. Transfer the browned bomboloni to a paper towel–lined plate or tray to drain. Roll in plenty of sugar and serve immediately while hot.

....

* If you do not have brioche à tête molds, these can successfully be made in a standard muffin pan. You will not get the same fluted edges, but they will still be great!

RECIPE NOTES

Other Uses for Brioche Dough

1. Roll into small, individual rolls, paint with egg wash, and dust with coarse sugar before baking. Bake and serve as a sweet bun along with a coffee.

2. On a generously floured surface, roll the dough into a rectangle, dust it with brown sugar, cinnamon, and nuts, and dot it with butter. Roll up the dough, slice it, and bake the slices for amazing cinnamon rolls.

3. Stud the dough with dried fruit, shards of chocolate, even cheese.

4. Roll the dough into small balls and place them in a buttered cake pan (like "monkey bread"). Drizzle the top with crème fraîche, scatter over some sliced almonds, and dust with sugar. Bake until browned—a messy, wonderfully sweet bread-meets-cake.

5. Bake in a loaf pan and use the bread for sandwiches.

6. Make round rolls and use for sandwiches, hamburgers, even ice cream.

Whole Wheat Scones with Currants

A tender scone is one of the most perfect vehicles for lots of butter and jam. At Buvette, we serve our scones with plenty of each and present the butter and jam right on the spoons we use to retrieve the condiments. Note that any dried fruit works well in these, I just happen to love currants! Chopped dried cherries or apricots would be especially nice.

[MAKES 8 SCONES]

½ cup currants

1½ cups unbleached all-purpose white flour

1½ cups whole wheat flour, plus extra for dusting

⅓ cup sugar

2 teaspoons baking powder

½ teaspoon baking soda

¾ teaspoon coarse salt

12 tablespoons (1½ sticks) cold unsalted butter, cubed

1 cup buttermilk, plus extra for brushing

¼ cup rolled oats

Preheat the oven to 400°F. Line a baking sheet with parchment paper.

Place the currants in a small bowl or mug, cover with very hot water, and set them aside to plump.

Meanwhile, whisk together the flours, sugar, baking powder, baking soda, and salt in a large mixing bowl. Add the butter and, using a pastry cutter or your fingertips, work it into the dry ingredients until the mixture is crumbly and the butter is evenly distributed. Drain the currants and stir them in with a wooden spoon. Stir in the buttermilk, and mix just until the dough comes together. Be careful not to overmix.

Dust the countertop with a bit of whole wheat flour and pat the dough into a rectangle that's an inch tall. At that height, your rectangle will be about 5 inches by 8 inches if you want to be specific, but there's no need to be that specific—these should be nice and rustic, really. Cut the dough into 8 squares and evenly space them out on the prepared baking sheet. Brush the top of each scone with a bit of buttermilk (incidentally, fingertips make for a great brush) and top each brushed scone with some of the oats.

Bake until the scones are evenly browned and smell buttery and wonderful, about 25 minutes. Serve warm.

Carrot Spoon Breads

This recipe, the ambrosia of carrot cakes, is adapted from *The Silver Palate Cookbook,* published in 1982. I bake the batter in individual ramekins and serve each with a generous spoonful of crème fraîche, which is actually plunged into the little cakes, hence the name spoon bread.

[MAKES 8 SPOON BREADS]

Butter, for greasing ramekins

1½ cups unbleached all-purpose flour, plus extra for the ramekins

2 carrots, peeled and roughly chopped

½ cup vegetable oil

2 large eggs, lightly beaten

⅓ cup drained canned crushed pineapple

1 teaspoon pure vanilla extract, if sugar isn't vanilla flavored

1 cup sugar, scented with spent vanilla pods (see page 241)

½ teaspoon coarse salt

1 teaspoon ground cinnamon

1½ teaspoons baking soda

¾ cup raw walnuts, roughly chopped

¾ cup shredded coconut

Crème fraîche, for serving

Preheat the oven to 350°F. Thoroughly butter and flour eight 4- to 6-ounce ramekins and set them aside.

Bring a pot of water to a boil and add the carrots. Cook until tender, about 15 minutes. Drain the carrots, place them in the bowl of a food processor, and blitz until they're roughly puréed. The mixture should measure ⅔ cup. If you have extra, set it aside for another use. In a small bowl, whisk together the carrot purée with the vegetable oil, eggs, pineapple, and vanilla extract, if using, and set the mixture aside.

Meanwhile, sift together the flour, sugar, salt, cinnamon, and baking soda in a large bowl. Whisk in the wet ingredients and stir in the walnuts and coconut.

Divide the batter evenly among the prepared ramekins and place them on a baking sheet, which makes it much easier to transfer them to and from the oven. Bake until the spoon breads are golden brown and a toothpick inserted into the center of one comes out clean, about 30 minutes. Let them cool at least 15 minutes (or up to a few hours) before topping each with a generous spoonful of crème fraîche. Once you've done that, serve immediately.

> RECIPE NOTE
> **On Seasonal Fruit Variations**
> Feel free to substitute mashed banana for the carrot purée. Persimmon purée is quite nice too, but if you use it, omit the pineapple and the coconut and substitute olive oil for vegetable oil.

Ricotta Fritters

Made with an incredibly simple-to-prepare batter, these fritters are light and crunchy and not too sweet. If you can get your hands on ricotta made from sheep's or goat's milk, by all means substitute it. And feel free to try any combination of nuts and dried fruit instead of the pine nuts and currants, or go minimal and leave them out altogether.

[MAKES ABOUT 20 FRITTERS]

1 cup (½ pound) high-quality whole milk ricotta cheese

½ cup unbleached all-purpose flour

Pinch coarse salt

1 teaspoon baking soda

½ teaspoon freshly grated nutmeg

2 large eggs, beaten together

2 tablespoons toasted pine nuts (optional)

2 tablespoons currants, soaked in hot water for 5 minutes and drained (optional)

Oil, for frying (corn, peanut, vegetable, canola, or grapeseed oil all work well)

Cinnamon-sugar, for serving

Stir together the ricotta, flour, salt, baking soda, nutmeg, and eggs, as well as the pine nuts and currants, if using.

Meanwhile, heat 2 inches of oil in a large, heavy pot over medium-high heat until it reaches 375°F, or until a pinch of flour sizzles on contact. Using 2 spoons, drop walnut-size spoonfuls of the fritter batter into the hot oil and fry, turning occasionally, until browned on all sides, about 5 minutes total. Do this in batches so that the pot is not crowded, and keep in mind that they will expand while they cook so be sure to keep plenty of room between them.

Transfer the browned fritters to a paper towel–lined baking sheet to drain while you continue frying the remaining batter.

Roll the fritters in plenty of cinnamon-sugar and serve immediately while warm.

Orange and Campari Marmalade

Making marmalade with just whole oranges and sugar cooked for a long time over a low flame is an old, very traditional method. The slow cooking allows all of the natural pectin to be coaxed from the oranges (pectin is what turns the marmalade thick and lovely). A splash of Campari adds not only color but also a most welcome, slightly bitter note. Keep in mind that the oranges should soak in water overnight so be sure to plan ahead.

[MAKES 2 CUPS MARMALADE]

1 pound juice oranges (or Cara Cara
or blood oranges), 4 to 5, washed well

1½ cups sugar

1½ ounces (3 tablespoons) Campari

Prick the oranges a few times with a fork and place them in a large bowl or container of water. Let the oranges soak overnight, changing the water once or twice. This will help release some of the bitterness.

Cut each orange in half and then cut each half into thin half-moons. Remove and discard all the seeds.

Place the sliced oranges into a heavy saucepan and add the sugar and Campari. Set the pot over low heat and cook, stirring occasionally, for 3 hours. The oranges will release lots of liquid and the mixture will become concentrated and thick.

Transfer the marmalade to a large jar. Let the marmalade cool to room temperature, then cover the jar and refrigerate for up to a month or two. (Discard if any mold forms, but this is very unlikely and easily avoided if the marmalade is kept covered and refrigerated.)

You can also can the marmalade in sanitized jam jars according to the instructions usually found with the jars (which are sold in hardware stores), or check out freshpreserving.com for detailed instructions.

Beurre Composé

Honey butter—the combination of butter, honey, bee pollen, and orange—is one of my favorite composed butters for breakfast time. Keep it in the refrigerator and serve it on just about anything, including toast, seeded crackers, pancakes, waffles, croissants, and scones. It's also lovely topped with candied fruits, especially citrus. At some good Italian markets you can find whole candied clementines that are stunning.

[MAKES 1½ CUPS COMPOSED BUTTER]

1 orange

12 tablespoons (1½ sticks) unsalted butter, preferably cultured butter, at room temperature

2 tablespoons bee pollen

⅓ cup honey

Pinch coarse salt

Remove the zest from the orange in large strips with a vegetable peeler. Cut the zest into small pieces, roughly the size of rice grains, which is to say fine, but not minuscule. Reserve the rest of the orange for another use (e.g., make yourself a small glass of juice). Place the butter in a bowl and mash with a fork, whisk, or potato masher. Mash in the orange zest, bee pollen, honey, and salt. Keep mashing until all of the ingredients are combined, but not too smooth. Shaped into a log, wrapped in plastic wrap, and refrigerated, this butter will keep for about a month.

> ### Thoughts on Translation and Composed Butter
> *In French there's no word for "cheap." There's just* pas cher, *"not expensive" or* bon marché, *"good deal." There's something wonderful about the absence of a negative word. I try to keep this way of phrasing things in mind. In this compound butter, for example, I like the butter and the additions to end up being not completely emulsified (that way, each bite looks and tastes a bit different, the irregular texture offering contrast and variation). And instead of using the obvious, slightly off-putting description "chunky," we simply call it "not too smooth." And just as the texture is random, so are the contents. Butter mixed with parsley and lemon is called* beurre maître d'hôtel, *a classic French composed butter often used as a topping for steak. I like to add roasted garlic to that too. Another favorite is equal amounts of butter worked into equal amounts of Roquefort, the result of which is excellent on steak. Or use it as a spread for toast, on its own, or underneath roasted figs or plums.*

Buttermilk Waffles
and Waffle Sandwiches

Weekend mornings at Buvette can be chaotic, and they demand a lot of stamina from my staff. I started making breakfast sandwiches on waffles for my hungry waiters before the brunch hordes arrived, and they have become not only a staff favorite but also a popular "off-the-menu" item for many of our regulars. Note that the batter must rest, so plan ahead.

[MAKES EIGHT 4-INCH-SQUARE WAFFLES; ENOUGH FOR 4 SANDWICHES]

2 large eggs	1 tablespoon sugar
1¾ cups buttermilk	1 tablespoon baking powder
½ cup vegetable oil or melted butter, plus more for greasing the waffle iron	Pinch coarse salt
	Powdered sugar, for serving
2 cups unbleached all-purpose flour	Unsalted butter, for serving
	Maple syrup, for serving

In a large bowl, whisk the eggs, buttermilk, and vegetable oil or butter together. Stir in the flour, sugar, baking powder, and salt and mix thoroughly. Cover the bowl with plastic wrap and refrigerate the batter for at least 30 minutes before using. At this point, the batter can be refrigerated for up to 3 days before using.

Preheat a waffle iron and lightly grease it with vegetable oil or butter. Ladle in as much batter as is appropriate depending on your waffle iron and cook until the waffles are golden brown. Remove the waffles from the iron. Eat as they are with powdered sugar, extra butter, and/or maple syrup or, ideally, use the waffles to make sandwiches.

BREAKFAST SANDWICHES

1. My first choice is a sunny-side-up egg with bacon and Jack cheese in between one halved waffle dripping with butter, bacon fat, and maple syrup. In a small pan, fry two strips of bacon, and when it's just crisp, crack your egg on top and fry it in the bacon fat directly on top of the bacon. When the egg is nearly cooked, cover it with a slice of cheese and cover the pan so that the cheese melts. Transfer the entire bacon-egg-cheese moment to half a waffle, drizzle with maple syrup, and cover with the second waffle half.

2. My second choice is a "PBS," which is chunky peanut butter with slices of fresh banana and strawberries in between waffles. The trick is to mix the peanut butter with equal parts butter, which makes the sandwich that much more decadent. I like my PBS dusted with powdered sugar.

3. Other favorite waffle sandwiches include Nutella and bananas, or scrambled eggs with spinach, roasted tomatoes, and Parmigiano-Reggiano cheese.

Toasted Oatmeal Brûlée

Roasting the dry oats before cooking them in water gives this oatmeal a nutty flavor that permeates each bite. The real pièce de résistance, however, is the caramelized sugar that gives this hot cereal a crème "brûlée-esque" top that's simply irresistible. Note this can be made up to a week in advance, making it especially great for when you're entertaining. Simply warm it in a 400°F oven for about 15 minutes before brûléing the top.

[SERVES 4]

2 cups jumbo rolled oats

4 cups water

1 teaspoon coarse salt

¼ cup pumpkin seeds

¼ cup sunflower seeds

¼ cup flaxseeds
(golden, brown, or a mix
of the two)

¼ cup ground hemp seeds

¼ cup raisins

¼ to ½ cup sugar

2 tablespoons bee pollen,
for serving

Warm milk, for serving

Preheat the oven to 425°F.

Place the oats on a baking sheet and bake, stirring the oats occasionally, until they smell toasty and are golden brown, about 10 minutes. Keep the oven on.

Meanwhile, bring the water to a boil in a large, heavy saucepan. Transfer the baked oats to the water along with the salt and stir to combine. Lower the heat and simmer until the oats are softened and thickened, about 10 minutes. Stir in all of the seeds and the raisins and transfer the mixture to a baking dish or a pie dish.

Place the dish in the oven and bake until all of the excess liquid has evaporated and the top is lightly browned and just firm to the touch, 10 to 15 minutes.

Remove the oatmeal from the oven and turn the oven from bake to broil.

Evenly sprinkle the sugar over the surface of the oatmeal, using at least ¼ cup and up to ½ cup if you like it especially sweet. Place the dish on a rack set 4 to 6 inches under the broiler and cook, with a watchful eye, until the sugar has melted and caramelized, and is nearly, but not entirely, burned. Carefully remove the oatmeal from the broiler and serve immediately with the bee pollen sprinkled on top, if you'd like.

Serve hot with a pitcher of warm milk alongside, if desired.

RECIPE NOTES

1. You can skip the broiler and use a kitchen torch to brûlé the sugar. Or, alternatively, you can place a metal spoon directly into the flame of a gas burner set on high heat and heat the spoon for at least a few minutes, or until it's red hot. Carefully holding the handle with a kitchen towel or oven mitt, place the spoon directly on the sugar and stand back—it will smoke!

2. Use any combination of nuts, seeds, and dried fruit that you'd like.

Yogurt Parfaits

This breakfast could not be simpler. Requiring no cooking whatsoever, it's a reminder that simple food can be really special when presented beautifully. Keep in mind that the nuts and honey can be placed into a jar, covered, and kept in a dark, cool spot for up to a few months. Use not only for layering with yogurt but also as a topping for ice cream or plain cake, or serve with cheese.

[SERVES 4]

1 cup nuts (I like a mixture of pine nuts, hazelnuts, pistachios, almonds, and walnuts, but use whatever you prefer), lightly toasted

⅓ cup honey

Pinch coarse salt

2 cups (16 ounces) plain Greek yogurt

Stir together the nuts, honey, and salt. In four clear serving vessels (juice glasses and empty jam jars both work well), evenly layer the nut-honey mixture with the yogurt in multiple layers, using about 1 inch of yogurt to ½ inch of the nut-honey mixture, depending on the size of your vessels. If you do use jam jars, you can put a lid on each parfait and store them in the refrigerator until you're ready to serve. Or take them with you in a cooler for a wonderful breakfast picnic.

Poached Winter Fruits

Use whatever combinations of dried fruits you'd like for this, including apricots, cherries, plums, apples, prunes, ginger, or golden raisins. There's no wrong decision here. Serve the fruits warm for breakfast or brunch, as an accompaniment for cheese, or even as dessert. A spoonful of yogurt, crème fraîche, or even ice cream would be wonderful adornments, though the fruit does stand well on its own.

[SERVES 4]

2 Bosc pears

3 cups dry white wine

2 cups sugar

Zest of 1 orange, removed in
large strips with a vegetable peeler

1 bay leaf

3 cups water

1½ cups mixed dried fruit

Peel the pears and cut them in half. Using a paring knife or a teaspoon, remove and discard the seeds and stem from each pear half and set the pears aside.

Meanwhile, combine the white wine, sugar, orange zest, and bay leaf in a large saucepan along with the water. Bring the mixture to a boil, then turn the heat to low so the liquid is just at a gentle simmer.

Add the pears to the poaching liquid and cook until they're tender, about 15 minutes. To test for doneness, insert a paring knife into one of the pear halves—it should be able to go through with barely any resistance.

Add the dried fruit to the pot and cook until they're warm and slightly plump, just another 5 minutes. Serve the pears and fruit warm in shallow bowls with some of their cooking liquid.

Summer Fruit Salad

When I was growing up in California, fresh fruit was in abundance, and a colorful salad was sometimes dinner. It's impossible to give an exact recipe for a great fruit salad since it depends entirely on the quality of your fruit and what's available. I love a mix of whatever I can get my hands on, including all varieties of melon, papaya, mango, pineapple, green and red plums, kiwi, fresh apricots and cherries, and all sorts of berries. Peel, seed, and trim the fruit as necessary and cut into pieces that are neither too small nor too big. You don't want each bite to taste the same (which is what happens when the fruit is cut too small), but you don't want to have to cut the fruit while you're eating it or struggle to get a bite (which is what happens when the fruit is cut too big). Squeeze fresh orange juice over the fruit salad when you serve it and also spoon over the contents of a passion fruit if you can find one. The fresh juices naturally sweeten the fruit salad, ensuring that each bite is well seasoned and juicy.

Classic 1930 Bloody Marys

Remember the mixing rule: clear cocktails are shaken and not-clear cocktails are stirred or rolled. Rolling is pouring all the ingredients from one glass into another and back, which is a very nice way to make your Bloody Mary. This recipe is the totally classic version we use at Buvette, where brunch is incomplete without at least one Bloody Mary.

[MAKES 4 DRINKS]

32 ounces (4 cups) tomato juice

2 tablespoons Pickled Horseradish (page 263) or prepared horseradish

1 tablespoon Worcestershire sauce

1 teaspoon celery salt

1 teaspoon coarse salt

About 20 dashes Tabasco sauce

Juice of 1 lemon

8 ounces (1 cup) vodka

An additional lemon cut into wedges, tender celery stalks, freshly ground black pepper, olives, and caperberries, for serving

In a large pitcher or container, stir together the tomato juice, horseradish, Worcestershire, celery salt, coarse salt, Tabasco, and lemon juice.

Fill 4 glasses generously with ice and evenly divide the tomato mixture among the glasses. Add 2 ounces (¼ cup) vodka to each glass and either stir or roll the contents together.

Squeeze a lemon wedge into each drink and drop the wedge into the glass. Garnish each with a stalk or two of celery, a grind of black pepper, and some olives and caperberries.

Green Tomato Bloody Marys

A refreshing twist on a Bloody Mary cocktail, this classic combines green tomatoes, celery, scallions, and cucumber. Not only an amazing color, the mixture, which is basically a very smooth gazpacho, also tastes bright and incredible. Note that you can make the mixture up to two days in advance—just be sure to give it a good stir before serving.

[MAKES 4 DRINKS]

4 large green tomatoes, stemmed

1 celery stalk, plus additional stalks (preferably from the inside of the celery), for serving

2 scallions, root ends and dark green tops trimmed off and discarded

1 small, unpeeled Persian cucumber, ends trimmed off and discarded

2 large fresh basil leaves

1 tablespoon Pickled Horseradish (page 263) or prepared horseradish (or substitute one-quarter of a fresh, seeded jalapeño)

2 teaspoons coarse salt

Juice of 1 lemon

½ teaspoon freshly ground white pepper

8 ounces (1 cup) vodka

Lemon or lime wedges, for serving

Mint leaves, for serving

Roughly dice the tomatoes, celery, scallions, and cucumber and place in a blender or food processor along with the basil, horseradish, salt, lemon juice, and white pepper. Process until completely smooth. If you'd like a particularly refined drink, you can pass this mixture through a sieve, but this is by no means necessary.

To serve, fill 4 glasses generously with ice and evenly divide the green tomato mixture among the glasses. Add 2 ounces (¼ cup) vodka to each glass and either stir or roll the contents together.

Garnish each drink with a lemon or lime wedge, a tender stalk of celery, and some mint leaves.

PART 2.

COFFEE AND TEA

Coffee and Tea

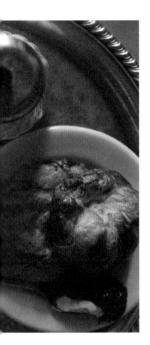

If Buvette were a sports car, our espresso machine would be the engine. Our bar is built around it and we put it to use constantly, whether for cappuccinos and caffè lattes in the morning, or for short shots of espresso after lunch or dinner. Similarly, our samovar (a beautiful Russian water heater similar to an electric tea kettle) is always on duty. In the winter, it's often filled with warm wine packed with spices for Vin Brûlé (page 154), but otherwise it's our constant supply of hot water, so we're ready to brew a cup of tea or a tisane (page 63) whenever a guest might want one.

The heartbeat of Buvette, coffee and tea fuel us—and not just literally. What I love most about coffee and tea are the rituals and objects that come with them: the silver teapots, the intense focus of the baristas, the smell of ground coffee beans, the milk and steam combining to make foam and, even more, seeing the milk swirl its way through a clear glass filled with ice and cold-brewed coffee.

I adore walking to McNulty's, the coffee and tea store on Christopher Street just around the corner, where I fill brown paper bags with dried chamomile flowers and golden Assam leaves. The names of all of the teas are intoxicating and the stamps they have to label your bags are so aged and beautiful. The dialogue I have with the shopkeepers is always inspiring. It feels good to have access to a place where history is so apparent; a place where the same scales have been weighing orders for generations. I count myself lucky that it's just at my doorstep.

Not unlike the salty snacks that come with cocktails in the evening, the food that accompanies coffee and tea adds to the pleasure of drinking them. In France, coffee is served with a little plate of sweets called *le café gourmand*. A wonderful tradition, I covet the whole assortment of small delights, which are referred to as *mignardises* (see pages 236–238 for some of my favorites). I especially love that the mignardises come automatically; there's no menu to choose from or decision to make. It's just understood that taking a moment to have a coffee is made better with a little something to eat—as is most everything, come to think of it.

Coffees

Espresso beans are no different from regular coffee beans (though they're usually very rich on the coffee bean flavor scale). The difference lies in the brewing method. While coffee is made by dripping boiling water through ground beans, espresso is made by packing the ground beans under pressure and forcing boiling water through them. A concentrated, powerful dose of coffee in compact form, espresso is the *buvette* of the coffee world, as I like to think of it.

AMERICANO
An espresso extended with hot water.

MACCHIATO
An espresso topped with a small amount of steamed milk.

CORTADO
From the Spanish word *cortar,* meaning "to cut," a cortado is an espresso cut with a small amount of steamed milk. I like to think of it as halfway between a macchiato and a cappuccino.

CAPPUCCINO
An espresso topped with a small amount of steamed milk and also topped with foam from the steamed milk. When I was a teenager, my dad and I would sometimes take a walk to Mario's Cigar Shop for cappuccinos after dinner. We'd argue about how to drink them—whether to stir the sugar in or let it sit and settle and become another thing altogether at the bottom of your cup. Little did I know we were both *wrong* because real Italians only drink cappuccinos in the morning—never in the evening, and especially not after dinner!

LATTE
An espresso topped with a large amount of steamed milk.

SHAKERATO
Sweeten a hot espresso with as much sugar as you'd like, pour it into a cocktail shaker filled with tons of ice, and shake vigorously as you would a martini. Strain into a glass and drink immediately. It will have a handsome layer of *espuma,* or foam, on top, like the head on a beer. This is a good thing. For a "New Yorker," shake it with milk and pour it, ice and all, into a glass.

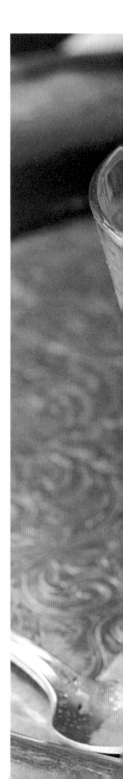

BICERIN

This drink is originally from Torino. Shave or grate 1 ounce of bittersweet chocolate and place it into the bottom of a small coffee cup. Pour over a fresh, hot shot of espresso, let it sit for a moment to allow the chocolate to melt, then stir the two together. Serve topped with a slick of cream that you've lightly sweetened and beaten so it's just starting to thicken, and a bit of extra shaved chocolate on top too. Serve with Almond Toffee (page 237).

Cold-Pressed Coffee

For the best, not to mention easiest, iced coffee, stir 1 cup of coarsely ground coffee together with 6 cups of cold water in a large jar. Cover the jar and let the mixture steep overnight at room temperature.

The next day, strain the mixture through a coffee filter or a sieve lined with cheesecloth into a bowl or another jar. Fill a glass with plenty of ice and pour over the strained coffee mixture. Add frothed milk, if you'd like. The strained coffee mixture can be stored in the refrigerator for up to a few days.

Staff Masala Chai

When powerful Hurricane Sandy hit New York in 2012, Buvette, like the rest of downtown Manhattan, lost power. One of the first things I did was make big vats of this chai on our gas stove for the staff to drink in an effort to use up our milk. Just a little spicy and totally warming (literally and figuratively), it was just what we needed to get us through the beginning of some unexpectedly daunting days.

[SERVES 4]

4 whole cloves

6 cardamom pods

1 teaspoon whole black peppercorns

2 bay leaves

2 tablespoons loose Assam black tea (or contents from 4 teabags)

1 teaspoon ground ginger

1 teaspoon ground cinnamon

Pinch coarse salt

¼ cup sugar

2 cups whole milk

2 cups water

Place the cloves, cardamom, peppercorns, bay leaves, and tea into a mortar and gently crush with the pestle. Alternatively, you can pulse the ingredients in a food processor or a coffee grinder.

Place the mixture into a saucepan and stir in the ginger, cinnamon, salt, sugar, and milk. Add the water and set the pot over medium-high heat. Bring the mixture to a boil, lower the heat, and simmer for 15 minutes. Strain the chai and serve hot.

The Perfect Cup

Patience is one ingredient that is necessary, but often elusive, in cooking. Patience can produce nuanced flavors in a slowly cooked soup and can make brioche light and airy. Patience can even make a simple cup of tea perfect. Teas, like coffee and chocolate, are greatly affected by their soil, elevation, and harvest. I prefer a good-quality, loose tea like golden Assam from Northern India.

For perfect tea:

1. Use 1 teaspoon of tea leaves for every cup of water.

2. Always bring the water to a rolling boil; a full 212°F.

3. Warm your teacups and teapot by rinsing them with a splash of boiling water before steeping.

4. Let the tea steep in a teapot for 3 to 5 minutes.

5. Strain the tea into your warmed teacups.

6. Add cold milk to your hot tea and let rest for 2 minutes before stirring together and enjoying. Milk brings out the toffee aromas and sweetness in the tea.

Collecting with the Table in Mind

I enjoy flea markets and yard sales, looking at history through others' belongings. In fact, I have been nicknamed "Rust and Dust." Seriously! I think it's incredible how you can find spoons from the Civil War, ashtrays from bygone hotels, baskets that were woven a hundred years ago—and all those things can have a place at the table.

Found objects add stories to a meal. They make guests curious and inspire playful, energetic dialogue. If an object speaks to you, even if it doesn't have an obvious purpose, buy it. It will find its way somewhere unexpected—an old trophy can become a vase for flowers, a pedestal candy dish can add height to your table and hold a plate of something delicious, a funky chair can be reserved for the guest of honor, a willow basket can become the perfect place to store your corks.

Some of my favorite antiques markets:

⊙ *Brimfeld Antique Show, Brimfeld, Massachusetts: May, July, and August*

⊙ *Brookyln Flea, Brooklyn, New York: Every Saturday and Sunday*

⊙ *Sparks Flea Market, Sparks, Kansas: May and September*

⊙ *Pasadena City College Flea Market, Pasadena, California: First Sunday of every month*

⊙ *Rose Bowl Flea Market, Pasadena, California: Second Sunday of every month*

Tisanes

A *tisane* refers to any hot, steeped drink that, unlike tea, does not have caffeine and is typically made with fresh or dried herbs, flowers, spices, seeds, berries, barks, and fruit. A tisane can be as simple as a *canarino*, which is simply lemon peel steeped in hot water, often served after dinner in Italy, and said to be good for digestion. Or a tisane can be a combination of flavors, such as lemon verbena mixed with fresh ginger and orange peel, or a warming combination of hibiscus flowers with apple, cinnamon sticks, and cardamom. Tisanes can even be medicinal if you use ingredients like burdock root and milk thistle, both good for your liver. Any dry tisane mixture, such as a combination of dried mint and rosemary, can be packed into a jar and makes a wonderful gift.

Drinking a tisane is a chance to pause, relax, and escape—a way to take your system and mind out of a cloud. To make a tisane, simply place whatever herbs or ingredients you are using into any kind of strainer you have: a metal tea ball, a silver strainer, an infuser spoon (which looks like two perforated spoons clamped together), or even a clean cotton sock. Place the device into a teacup or teapot. Wet the ingredients with a bit of cold water before pouring hot water over and let it steep however long you desire, at least 1 minute for a light brew and up to 10 minutes for a strong, robust one.

PART 3.

AFTERNOONS

Buvette / The Pleasure of Good Food

Afternoons

Sometimes I have a sixth sense that tells me not to leave home without a bit of nourishment. This is especially true on sunny afternoons when I don't know where the day might take me. Once when I was working for a brief time in Australia, some friends and I planned to go horseback riding in the rainforest outside of Sydney. Getting to the horses required a few hours of travel, and before we left the house, I realized no one had mentioned anything about lunch. The only food we had in our sparsely populated refrigerator was a lonely zucchini and some eggs. I quickly made a frittata, cut it into pieces, and put them between slices of bread. I wrapped the sandwiches in waxed paper and put them in my bag. The horseback riding was a wild adventure and completely exhilarating until we all realized we were dehydrated from the hot sun and were starving. Never in my life has anything tasted better than that sandwich.

Anytime you leave the house you have the opportunity for a picnic, whether it's planned or spontaneous. Even if you're not eating outside, lunchtime is a wonderful chance to pause from a busy day. The following pages include the drinks, salads, vegetables (including a whole section on artichokes), pizzas, and soups that are best for daytime eating. It also includes my version of a *croque-monsieur*, arguably the second best sandwich in the world.

A FEW AFTERNOON MENUS

PICNIC LUNCH FOR A WARM DAY

Panaché

Roast Chicken Salad and Haricots Verts with Mustard Dressing

Heirloom Tomato Salad with Cucumbers and Bread

Carottes Râpées with Pistachios and Coriander Vinaigrette

Cold Steamed Artichokes with Mayonnaise

BOOK CLUB LUNCH AT HOME

Bibonade

Pinzimonio

Soupe au Pistou

Pissaladière

SNOW DAY LUNCH FOR KIDS

Old-Fashioned Lemonade

Croque-Monsieurs

Croque-Monsieur

A beloved sandwich, a croque-monsieur is basically a grilled cheese as seen through a decadent French lens. A constant on my menu at Buvette, we serve plenty of these at lunch and also late at night when we put them back on the menu after eleven o'clock. They are great for a party since you can assemble a tray of croques ahead of time and simply pop them into the oven when guests arrive.

[MAKES 4 SANDWICHES]

1 recipe Béchamel Sauce (page 269)

2 tablespoons whole-grain mustard

8 slices bread

8 slices cooked ham, preferably prosciutto cotto

1 cup coarsely grated Gruyère cheese

1 teaspoon Herbes de Provence (page 261)

Preheat the oven to 425°F. Line a baking sheet with parchment paper.

Stir the béchamel together with the mustard and, dividing the mixture evenly, spread it on one side of each slice of bread, being sure to spread the béchamel from corner to corner on each slice.

On 4 of the prepared slices of bread, place 2 slices of ham directly on top of the béchamel and then sprinkle 2 tablespoons of the Gruyère on top of the ham. Place the remaining 4 béchamel-coated slices of bread on top of the Gruyère, béchamel side up. Place the 4 sandwiches onto the prepared baking sheet. Sprinkle each sandwich with a small pinch of herbes de Provence and 2 tablespoons of the remaining Gruyère. Place the sandwiches in the oven and bake until the cheese is totally melted and is starting to crisp, about 10 minutes.

CROQUE-FORESTIER

For vegetarian friends, make **Croque-Forestiers** by simply exchanging the ham for a handful of mushrooms that have been roasted with olive oil, salt, sage, and rosemary.

CROQUE-MADAME

To gild the lily, make **Croque-Madames** by placing a fried egg on top of each sandwich (works on any version of the sandwich). It should rest like a good hat, leaning *just so.*

Schiacciata Dough

Schiacciata is similar to the ubiquitous focaccia and depending how the dough is handled, it can be stretched into a thin pizza crust or into thicker focaccia. It's best to let the dough rise slowly, ideally overnight in the refrigerator. That way the yeast, which is essentially marinating in the dough, can develop as much flavor as possible, and create that desirable airy effect.

[MAKES ENOUGH DOUGH FOR ONE HALF SHEET PAN
OR TWO 12-INCH INDIVIDUAL PIZZAS]

3 cups unbleached all-purpose flour

1½ teaspoons active dry yeast

1½ cups room-temperature water, plus more as needed

1 teaspoon coarse salt

2 tablespoons extra-virgin olive oil, plus more as needed

In the bowl of a stand mixer fitted with the dough hook (or by hand; see Recipe Note page 72), combine 1½ cups of the flour with the yeast and 1 cup of the water and mix on low until just combined. Lift the dough hook out of the mixture and scrape down the sides of the bowl if necessary. This mixture is called a sponge and is the heart of your dough—it's where the yeast activates and transforms everything from ingredients into dough.

Blanket the sponge with the remaining 1½ cups flour, sprinkle with the salt, and drizzle with the olive oil. Turn the machine to medium speed to combine all of the ingredients, and then slowly pour in the remaining ½ cup water. You are looking for a wet, sticky dough that holds together just so, depending on your conditions (i.e., the humidity, your flour, etc.); add a bit more water if necessary. Once the dough begins to take form, turn the mixer to high and let it go until the dough is smooth and elastic, makes a slapping noise against the mixer bowl, and has formed around the dough hook, leaving the sides of the bowl quite clean. It will take a full 5 minutes.

Coat a large mixing bowl with a thin layer of olive oil, and transfer the dough to the bowl. Rub the surface of the dough with a bit more olive oil, and cover the bowl with plastic wrap. Let it sit until it has doubled in size, either a few hours at room temperature, or at least 12 hours in the refrigerator. It can sit in the refrigerator, covered with plastic wrap, for up to 3 days, or up to a month in the freezer. Defrost at room temperature before using. »CONTINUES

A Note on Technique

You can easily make this dough by hand if you (a) prefer to and/or (b) don't have a stand mixer. Simply combine the dough using a wooden spoon, and instead of letting the mixer knead the dough, knead it by hand on a floured surface, working hard to continually fold the dough over onto itself until it is smooth and elastic, at least 10 minutes.

The Infinite Variety of Schiacciata Dough

This dough is so versatile. I like to think of it as a blank canvas with endless possibilities. Its flexibility especially appeals to me because I always bake with my shirttail untucked, so to speak. Sometimes I spread the dough into a round, slash it a few times, dock it with olive oil, sprinkle it with chopped thyme, torn black olives, and salt, and place it into a hot oven. Other times I cut an orange into paper-thin slices, fan them over the dough, sprinkle them with fresh rosemary and red chili flakes, and then give the whole thing a drizzle of honey. Roasted grapes or shards of fall apples are wonderful too. See below for instructions on how to prepare more of my favorite variations.

SCHIACCIATA BIANCA

For the simplest **Schiacciata Bianca,** coat a half sheet pan with a generous pour of olive oil (about ¼ cup) and press the dough into the pan. The dough will be a bit stubborn when you first put it into the pan. Let it rest for about 20 minutes and then even it out with your fingertips. That final resting does wonders, and your patience will be rewarded. Drizzle a little bit more olive oil on top of the dough, and sprinkle with coarse salt and a few fresh rosemary leaves. Dimple the surface with your fingertips and send it into a 475°F oven until browned, about 20 minutes.

SCHIACCIATA OCCHIO DI BUE

Occhio di bue, "bull's eye," refers to the glorious egg that's cracked into the center of the partially cooked schiacciata and emerges with a runny yolk. Some of my other favorite toppings include a mixture of Gorgonzola cheese and pears, figs with prosciutto, and cèpes (porcini mushrooms) with walnuts. You can't go wrong, really.

For two occhio di bue, divide a batch of rested schiacciata dough in half. Using your hands and gravity, pull and stretch one half of the dough to form a pizza (don't worry about making it a perfect circle). At this point, if you have a grill or a grill pan, get it nice and hot and mark the pizza on either side. If you don't have a grill or a grill pan, place the shaped pizza dough onto an oiled sheet pan and send it into a 475°F oven until just barely beginning to brown, 5 to 10 minutes.

Drizzle a bit of olive oil on the parcooked pizza, and grate a thin layer of Parmigiano-Reggiano over the top. Crack an egg in the middle and return the pizza to the oven. Bake until the egg is set and the crust is nicely browned, about 10 minutes. Remove it from the oven, grate a little bit more cheese over the top, and scatter

a handful of arugula over the cheese. Drape some prosciutto over the pizza and serve it immediately. Repeat the process with the other half of the dough because (a) you have it and (b) one is never enough!

TARTE FLAMBÉE

Literally translated to "pie baked in the flames," *tarte flambée*, a classic Alsatian dish, is the most decidedly French way to treat the schiacciata dough. Basically a bacon-and-onion pizza with crème fraîche, you can cut the tarte flambée into bite-size pieces and serve it as a hors d'oeuvre with cocktails, or slice it into large wedges, accompany it with a salad, and call it lunch.

Generously coat a half sheet pan with olive oil and stretch and pull a batch of dough so that it fills the pan. Using your fingers, press the dough so that it forms a bit of a lip around all of the edges and the center is thinner. This will guarantee that once you load it with the onion mixture, the underside will cook through, plus it will give you a beautiful crust along the sides. Drizzle a bit of olive oil over the surface of the dough and rub it around with your fingers so that the whole thing has a nice sheen. Cover the dough with a clean kitchen towel and let it rest for at least 20 minutes while you prepare the onions.

Meanwhile, set a large skillet over high heat and, once it gets hot, add ½ pound of sliced bacon that you've cut into ½-inch-thick pieces to the pan. It should immediately smell incredible. Cook, stirring a bit, until the bacon starts to render its fat, 2 or 3 minutes. Add 2 sliced yellow onions to the pan, reduce the heat to medium-high, and cook, stirring occasionally, until the onions are soft and a little bit brown and the bacon is a tiny bit crisp, about 20 minutes. Season the mixture to taste with salt and pepper and set it aside.

Meanwhile, whisk together ½ cup of crème fraîche and ½ teaspoon of freshly grated nutmeg and season the mixture to taste with salt and pepper. Set it aside.

Uncover the dough and evenly spread the crème fraîche mixture over the middle of the dough, leaving the outer, higher edges bare. Pile the onion and bacon mixture on top of the crème fraîche.

Bake the tarte flambée in a 375°F oven until the crust is nicely browned and the onions have taken on more color and are tempting and crispy. Transfer to a wire rack and let it cool for at least 15 minutes before cutting and eating. Serve warm or at room temperature.

FRUIT FOCACCIA

Cover 2 cups of whatever dried fruit you'd like with hot water and let it sit until it's at room temperature. Drain the fruit, reserving both the fruit and the soaking liquid. Prepare the Schiacciata Dough per the instructions, measuring 1½ cups of the soaking liquid and using it instead of the water called for in the recipe. This liquid will both sweeten and color the dough. Once the dough has formed, knead »CONTINUES the softened dried fruit into the dough, place the dough into an oiled bowl, cover it with a tea towel, and let it rest and rise, about 1 hour.

Bake on a sheet pan, and serve squares of it alongside cheese. Alternatively, the focaccia can be cut into long slices and toasted, which yields slightly sweet, fruit-laden crackers. These are especially useful as a vehicle for Roquefort beurre composé (page 41).

Celery Root Rémoulade

This white-on-white, chic and classic bistro salad of raw, crunchy matchsticks of celery root dressed with mayonnaise and mustard is essentially the French version of coleslaw. I like serving it alongside rich foods like Pâté de Campagne (page 147), or as a side dish alongside a simple Roast Chicken (page 202). It's also wonderful as part of a lunch of composed salads.

[SERVES 4]

1 celery root, peeled
(about ¾ pound before peeling)

¼ cup mayonnaise
(preferably homemade, page 264)

1½ tablespoons Dijon mustard

2 teaspoons freshly squeezed lemon juice

2 teaspoons water

½ teaspoon coarse salt

½ teaspoon freshly ground black pepper

Cut the celery root lengthwise into thin slices, using a mandoline if possible to make this really uniform and easy. Pile the slices and cut them lengthwise into thin matchsticks. You should have about 2 cups of matchsticks.

Whisk together the mayonnaise, mustard, lemon juice, water, salt, and pepper in a large bowl and add the celery root. Toss to combine. The salad can be made up to a day ahead as long as you keep it in an airtight container in the refrigerator.

> **RECIPE NOTE**
>
> An unusual but tasty application for Celery Root Rémoulade is a sandwich made with fried skate. The combination merges two classic French dishes—pan-fried skate and celery root rémoulade—into one of my favorite things on earth, the fried fish sandwich, a specialty of East Coast seafood shacks.
>
> To make one, simply pan-fry a piece of skate in olive oil and serve it on toasted country bread with plenty of celery root rémoulade (it sort of takes the place of coleslaw) and also a generous swipe of Sauce Gribiche (page 264), some sliced radishes, and a handful of watercress. Be sure to serve this with lots of napkins, as eating it can get a bit messy—not necessarily a bad thing. Serve these with big glasses of Panaché (page 94), an icy beer with lemon.

Pinzimonio

Pinzimonio is an Italian crudité. It is both utterly simple and thoroughly sophisticated. Commonly eaten at the start of the meal, pinzimonio celebrates the arrival of the season's first pressing of olive oil. It is traditional to include every vegetable in season. Feel free to use whatever vegetables you love.

[SERVES 4]

2 heads endive

1 head Treviso or radicchio

1 bulb fennel

1 bunch scallions

1 bunch radishes

1 cup best extra-virgin olive oil

Coarse salt

Freshly ground black pepper

Remove the stem ends from the endive and the Treviso and separate the leaves.

Trim off and discard the tough base of the fennel (approximately the bottom ¼ inch) and any dark, bruised outer layers. Trim off most of the green tops and fronds and set aside for another use (or discard). Slice the fennel lengthwise into pieces that are neither too thick nor too thin.

Trim off and discard the root ends and the very dark green tops of the scallions.

Cut the radishes in half lengthwise, leaving a bit of their greens on top to act as handles.

You could also add cleaned and trimmed carrots, celery, tomatoes, green beans, asparagus, etc.

Artfully arrange all of the prepared vegetables on a platter, pour the olive oil into a shallow bowl, and season it with a pinch of salt and freshly ground black pepper. That is literally it.

A Secret for Menu Writing

When making a menu, memories are a great source of inspiration, but old cookbooks are useful too. Even travel guides inspire with their informative "where to eat" and "what not to miss" suggestions. They indicate the dishes you must not leave a place without trying; and, to me, those are the dishes I am most interested in not only consuming but also cooking.

Pan Bagnat

When you walk along the beach in Nice, you hear the echo of vendors shouting out *"Pan bagnat! Pan bagnat!"* to everyone within earshot, all hawking their own version of the favorite French tuna sandwich. While the tuna mixture makes a great sandwich, it's actually quite good on its own as a salad served on a bed of tender lettuce leaves. Don't be put off by the long list of ingredients—there's a lot of chopping, but zero cooking!

[SERVES 4]

Two 5-ounce cans imported Italian or Spanish tuna packed in oil, drained

2 roasted red bell peppers, stemmed, seeded, and diced

½ small cucumber, peeled and diced

1 small fennel bulb, outer leaves removed, cored and finely diced

½ red onion, peeled and finely diced

¼ cup black olives, pitted and roughly chopped

4 scallions, thinly sliced

1 celery stalk, finely diced

2 preserved artichokes, diced

1 tablespoon capers

1½ tablespoons Herbes de Provence (page 261)

½ teaspoon red chili flakes, plus more as needed

12 fresh basil leaves, torn into small pieces

Juice of 1 lemon, plus more as needed

⅓ cup extra-virgin olive oil

1 teaspoon coarse salt, plus more as needed

4 cups tender lettuce leaves

1 ripe tomato, thinly sliced

2 hard-boiled eggs, thinly sliced

12 high-quality, olive oil–packed anchovies

In a large bowl, combine the tuna, roasted peppers, cucumber, fennel, onion, olives, scallions, celery, artichokes, capers, herbes de Provence, chili flakes, basil, lemon juice, olive oil, and salt. Stir to combine and season the salad to taste with additional salt, chili flakes, and/or lemon, if you'd like.

Arrange the lettuce in an even layer on a large platter and place the tuna salad over the lettuce. Artfully arrange the sliced tomato, eggs, and anchovies over the tuna and serve immediately.

RECIPE NOTE

For a Sandwich...

Cut 6 crusty rolls nearly in half, leaving them attached at one end. Divide the tuna evenly among the rolls and pack the tops with the sliced tomato, egg, and anchovies. Wrap the sandwiches in parchment paper or waxed paper and give them each a good press before eating, encouraging all of that lovely oil to seep into the bread. The real prize in this sandwich is the olive oil–soaked bread.

Roast Chicken Salad
and Haricots Verts with
Mustard Vinaigrette

This salad has everything going for it: the cool greens against the warm chicken, the softness of the potatoes against the crisp chicken skin and the crunchy green beans, the richness of the chicken fat against the bite of mustard and vinegar. The perfect lunch, it is a dish I could happily eat every single day—it somehow feels light enough for the summer and substantial enough for the winter.

[SERVES 4]

8 small waxy potatoes

Coarse salt

¾ pound haricots verts (about 2 large handfuls), stem ends trimmed

4 large handfuls lovely salad greens (a mix of butter lettuce, endive, and watercress is nice)

Freshly ground black pepper

½ cup Vinaigrette (page 258)

1 tablespoon Dijon mustard

1 tablespoon whole-grain mustard

1 small Roast Chicken (page 202), still warm

2 radishes, thinly sliced

Place the potatoes in a saucepan, cover with cold water, and add a spoonful of salt. Bring to a boil and cook until the potatoes are tender, about 20 minutes. Using a slotted spoon, remove the potatoes from the cooking water and set them aside to cool; keep the cooking water at a boil. When cool enough to handle, peel the potatoes, break them in half, and set them aside.

Meanwhile, add the haricots verts to the cooking water and cook until they are just tender, about 5 minutes. Drain the haricots verts and transfer to a plate or bowl to cool.

Arrange the greens on a large platter and sprinkle them with salt and pepper. Whisk together the vinaigrette and the mustards and drizzle the greens with one-third of the dressing. Toss the potatoes and the green beans with another third of the dressing and lay them on top of the dressed greens. Tear all of the meat and skin from the chicken in large-ish pieces and scatter over the vegetables. Drizzle the whole thing with the remaining dressing, scatter the radishes over the top, and serve immediately.

On Setting the Table

I like to leave a stack of plates and a pile of folded napkins and a handful of silverware in the middle of the table and let everyone help themselves and one another. It's fun and informal, it lets your guests feel helpful, and it allows you to steal a few extra minutes in the kitchen.

Fava Bean Salad

My guests at Buvette start asking for this salad as soon as the snow melts. Shelling fava beans can be tedious, but this task's repetition can also be quite meditative. To shell favas, first remove the beans from their large pods. Place the beans in a pot of boiling water for just a minute, drain them, and let them cool to room temperature. Carefully peel away and discard the tough, pale layer from the outside of each tender, bright-green bean.

[SERVES 4]

2 tablespoons extra-virgin olive oil,
plus more as needed

2 cups freshly shelled fava beans (see note above)

1 fresh red chili, sliced, or pinch red chili flakes

1 garlic clove, finely minced or puréed on
a Microplane grater

Coarse salt

1 head escarole, cleaned and roughly chopped

Leaves from 3 sprigs fresh mint, roughly torn

Leaves from 4 sprigs fresh basil, roughly torn

1 lemon, plus more as needed

2 ounces pecorino Romano cheese,
thinly shaved

Heat the olive oil in a large skillet over medium-high heat. Add the fava beans, chili, garlic, and a large pinch of salt. Cook, stirring occasionally, until the favas have lost their raw bite and are bright green, about 5 minutes. Set the favas aside to cool.

Meanwhile, using your hands, mix the escarole, mint, and basil together in a large bowl. Once the favas are cool, add them to the escarole mixture and squeeze over the juice from the lemon. Gently combine all of the ingredients and add salt. Season with more lemon and more olive oil, if needed. Scatter over the shaved pecorino Romano and serve immediately.

Heirloom Tomato Salad with Cucumbers and Bread

Tomato salads depend entirely on your tomatoes and should only be made when the fruit is at its best. I like to add big, rustic croutons made with toasted bread that's been rubbed with garlic and well seasoned, then soaked with vinegar and water so they soften. Combined with crunchy cucumbers and fresh scallions and basil, this salad is substantial and full of texture and great summer flavor.

[SERVES 4]

2 pounds ripe heirloom tomatoes (a mixture of different shapes and colors is great)

Coarse salt

Freshly ground black pepper

4 scallions, sliced

½ English cucumber, chopped

¼ cup extra-virgin olive oil

3 tablespoons sherry vinegar

4 slices toasted country bread

1 garlic clove, peeled

2 cups water

Handful fresh basil leaves, torn

Cut the tomatoes into bite-size pieces. (Small cherry tomatoes can simply be halved while large tomatoes should be stemmed and cut into wedges; use your judgment.) Place the tomatoes in a bowl and season aggressively with salt and pepper. Add the scallions and cucumber and pour in the olive oil and 1 tablespoon of the sherry vinegar. Using your hands, gently toss all of the ingredients to combine.

Rub the toast with the garlic and season with salt and pepper. Place the remaining 2 tablespoons vinegar in a large bowl along with the water and dunk the bread into the mixture briefly just to soften the bread. Tear the bread into large pieces and combine them with the tomatoes in the bowl.

Arrange the salad on a large platter and scatter the torn basil over the top. Serve immediately.

Shaved Brussels Sprouts with Pecorino and Walnuts

Everyone who has this dish at Buvette asks what's in it, and can never believe how simple it is. I like small, irregular bits of cheese throughout this salad. It seems obvious that you should use a grater to easily cut small pieces of cheese, but I find the consistency of grated cheese bits too uniform and unpleasingly perfect. To achieve the right texture, simply twist the tines of a fork into a chunk of cheese, raking it as you go.

[SERVES 4]

2 dozen Brussels sprouts

½ cup raw walnut halves

¼ cup finely fork-crumbled pecorino Romano cheese (see note above)

2 tablespoons extra-virgin olive oil, plus more as needed

Pinch coarse salt

Trim off and discard the bottom ends of the sprouts and discard any loose or discolored outer leaves. Using a mandoline, the slicing attachment on a food processor, or simply a sharp knife, carefully shave the sprouts. Combine them in a large bowl with the remaining ingredients, scrunching the sprouts with your hands as you mix so that they wilt a little. Season to taste with more salt, if necessary, and a bit more olive oil if you think it needs it; the exact amount will depend not only on your preference, but also the size of the Brussels sprouts.

Endive and Radicchio Salad
with Pears, Pomegranate, Walnuts, and Roquefort

The radicchio in this gorgeous salad can be swapped for *castelfranco,*
one of the most beautiful lettuces in the whole world. A cross between
red-leafed chicory and endive, it's pale green with red specks the color
of wine. It is not always easy to find, so jump on it if you see it, but
absolutely feel free to substitute easier-to-find radicchio in its place.

[SERVES 4]

1 head endive, leaves separated

1 fistful watercress leaves

1 small head castelfranco or radicchio, torn

1 Bosc pear, stemmed, cored, and sliced

⅓ cup extra-virgin olive oil

2 tablespoons balsamic vinegar

Coarse salt

¼ cup fresh pomegranate seeds

¼ cup roughly chopped walnuts

½ cup crumbled Roquefort or other blue cheese

Arrange all of the lettuces artfully on a large platter or in a bowl. Scatter the pear
slices over the lettuces and drizzle the whole salad evenly with the olive oil and then
the balsamic vinegar. Give it a good pinch of salt. Scatter the pomegranate seeds,
walnuts, and cheese over the top and serve immediately.

Zucchini and Pecorino with Mint

I learned of this salad from Rita Sodi, who runs the fine restaurant I Sodi on Christopher Street, just around the corner from Buvette. It's the best thing to make when you're confronted with too much zucchini in the summertime. Not only is it quick to throw together but also incredibly beautiful with its long, thin ribbons of zucchini interrupted with shards of cheese and perfectly imperfect torn mint leaves.

[SERVES 4]

2 large or 3 medium zucchini, ends trimmed

Leaves from 4 sprigs fresh mint, torn

½ fresh red chili, thinly sliced

2 ounces pecorino Romano cheese, thinly sliced

¼ cup high-quality extra-virgin olive oil

Coarse salt

Freshly ground black pepper

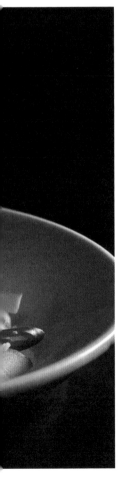

Using a mandoline, vegetable peeler, or a sharp knife, slice the zucchini lengthwise into long ribbons. On a serving platter or on each of four individual plates, arrange them so that they have some height, folding them here and there so that they rest on one another and stand up a bit. Scatter the torn mint, red chili, and cheese over the zucchini, and drizzle with the olive oil. Season the salad with plenty of salt and pepper and serve immediately.

Mushrooms, Shaved Celery, and Parmigiano-Reggiano

This salad is all about the beauty of the randomness. I like to think of it as an ode to Andy Goldsworthy, the inspiring British artist who makes sculptures out of natural materials, often set in nature. I take my time composing each serving so it looks both stylish and earthy and season not only the vegetables, but the plate too. This technique ensures that each bite is surrounded by flavor.

[SERVES 4]

2 celery stalks

Small handful tender celery leaves

2 shallots, peeled and very thinly sliced

6 large button mushrooms (if you can find fresh porcini mushrooms, use them!)

2 ounces Parmigiano-Reggiano cheese

Extra-virgin olive oil

Coarse salt

Freshly ground black pepper

Cut the celery in half crosswise and then thinly slice the pieces lengthwise on a mandoline so you have beautiful, crunchy celery ribbons. Place the sliced celery, celery leaves, and shallots in a bowl of icy-cold water for a few minutes, then lift them onto paper towels to drain. This step will help take the bite out of the shallots and crisp the celery.

Meanwhile, thinly slice the mushrooms and the cheese using a mandoline or a sharp knife and set them aside.

Drizzle each of four salad plates, or one large serving dish, with a little olive oil and sprinkle with a pinch of salt and a few grinds of black pepper. Lay down the mushrooms in a single layer and then artfully and casually arrange the celery, celery leaves, shallots, and cheese on top of the mushrooms. Drizzle everything with a bit more olive oil, and season with a final pinch of salt and a few more grinds of black pepper. Serve immediately.

Carottes Râpées
with Pistachios and
Coriander Vinaigrette

This salad, a riff on a French classic, *carottes râpées,* allows me to sneak in coriander in two ways, first with roughly crushed seeds that have been toasted and second with fresh cilantro, the plant that grows from coriander seeds. Rounded out with pistachios and an assertive lemon dressing, this salad is bright in both color and flavor.

[SERVES 4]

2 tablespoons freshly squeezed lemon juice

1 small garlic clove, finely minced or
puréed on a Microplane grater

⅓ cup extra-virgin olive oil

Pinch coarse salt

Pinch red chili flakes

¾ teaspoon coriander seeds, toasted

1 pound carrots, peeled and coarsely grated
(about 3 cups grated)

¼ cup shelled pistachios

Small handful fresh cilantro leaves

In a large bowl, whisk together the lemon juice, garlic, olive oil, salt, and chili flakes. Using the flat side of your knife blade or a mortar and pestle, gently crush the coriander seeds and add them to the dressing. Stir the carrots and pistachios into the dressing, then gently stir in the cilantro. Let the salad sit for at least half an hour before serving. The salad will keep, well covered, in the refrigerator for a few days.

Yellow Wax Beans
with Basil Pesto

While this dish calls for yellow wax beans, it is great with a variety of fresh beans, including thin green haricots verts, stunning purple string beans, and long, flat Romano beans. That said, the beans here are just a vehicle for basil pesto, the deliriously good herb sauce originally from Genoa in northern Italy.

[SERVES 4]

Coarse salt

1½ pounds yellow wax beans (about 2 large handfuls), stem ends trimmed

½ cup Basil Pesto (page 260)

2 tablespoons pine nuts, lightly toasted

2 tablespoons high-quality extra-virgin olive oil

Freshly ground black pepper

Bring a large pot of water to a boil and stir in a spoonful of salt.

Add the wax beans to the cooking water and remove them when they are just tender, about 5 minutes. Drain the beans and transfer to a plate or bowl to cool.

Combine the wax beans with the pesto and stir to evenly coat. Transfer to a serving platter. Scatter the pine nuts over the top, and drizzle with the olive oil. Season with a final sprinkle of salt and a few grinds of black pepper.

Warm Potatoes with Anchovies

The warm anchovy vinaigrette that bathes these potatoes is the exact mixture I use for Bagna Cauda (page 124) with the addition of vinegar and parsley. While I often use big, assertive flavors like horseradish, mustard, and vinegar, I like my vinaigrettes on the "soft" side, not too acidic. They should complement, not compete.

[SERVES 4]

A dozen new potatoes or small
Yukon Golds (about 1½ pounds)

⅓ cup extra-virgin olive oil

2 garlic cloves, peeled and crushed

8 high-quality, fat anchovy fillets

2 tablespoons sherry vinegar

Coarse salt

A dozen pieces Tomato Confit (page 266)

¼ cup roughly chopped fresh flat-leaf parsley leaves

½ cup Niçoise olives

Place the potatoes in a large pot of salted, cool water, and bring to a boil over high heat. Cook until they're tender, about 20 minutes.

Meanwhile, put the olive oil, garlic, and anchovies in a small saucepan over low heat to infuse and soften. Stir every so often, until the anchovies have dissolved into the oil and the garlic is soft, about 10 minutes. Be sure to keep the heat low so the garlic and olive oil do not burn. Remove the pot from the heat and mash the garlic into the oil with a fork. Set aside.

Drain the potatoes, transfer them to a serving platter, and while they're still warm, crush them lightly with a fork. Evenly drizzle them with the vinegar and sprinkle with salt. Spoon the anchovy dressing over the potatoes and serve, garnished with the Tomato Confit, parsley, and olives.

Old-Fashioned Lemonade

Just about the most refreshing drink in the world, every-one loves lemonade. At Buvette, there's no bottled lemon juice or simple syrup for us. We make each glass to order and stir freshly squeezed lemon juice with sugar right in the glass we're going to serve it in and fill it with plenty of ice and sparkling water so it's got a little fizz.

[MAKES 1 LEMONADE; EASILY MULTIPLIED]

2 tablespoons freshly squeezed lemon juice

2 tablespoons superfine sugar

Ice

Sparkling water

Stir the lemon juice and sugar together in a tall glass until the sugar has dissolved. Fill the glass with ice and top off with about ½ cup sparkling water. Stir to combine and serve immediately.

    Lemonice: Old-Fashioned Lemonade with a few dashes of bitters.

    Lemonari: Old-Fashioned Lemonade with a shot of Campari.

SHANDIES

    Panaché: ⅓ cup Old-Fashioned Lemonade and ⅔ cup beer, preferably one that's blonde in color and light in flavor, over ice.

    Monaco: Same as the above, but with a splash of grenadine.

Bibonade

Bibonade is a word I coined for a refreshing combination of fruit and wine served over ice that can be made even lighter and more effervescent when topped off with sparkling wine or water. I first learned about it when I lived and worked in Italy and we had wine mixed with water every day at lunch. I rediscovered it when I visited France and learned that rosé is always served over ice during the summertime. While some would think these combinations would dilute the wine or make it lose its integrity, I would suggest just thinking about it as a whole other thing altogether. My favorite bibonade combinations include sliced apricots in Muscadet, halved green grapes in Riesling, sliced black plums in rosé, and sliced yellow plums in white wine.

Raw Artichoke Salad

Artichokes are my favorite vegetable in the entire world, and not everyone knows that you can eat them raw. A lesson in simplicity, this salad is emblematic of the phrase "if it's not broken, don't fix it." Here, thinly sliced artichokes are dressed only with olive oil and fresh lemon juice and adorned with Parmigiano-Reggiano and nothing else. It's simple and perfect.

[SERVES 4]

8 small artichokes

2 lemons

Extra-virgin olive oil

Coarse salt

2 ounces shaved Parmigiano-Reggiano cheese

Working with one artichoke at a time, hold on to the stem of the artichoke and remove the dark green outer leaves, one by one, to reveal the tender yellow leaves. Turn the artichoke around and, while holding on to the yellow leaves, use a potato peeler to clean away the tough, dark green skin from the stem. Halve one of the lemons and rub each of the artichokes with the cut side of one of the lemon halves. Fill a large bowl with water and squeeze in the remaining juice from the lemon half as well as the juice from the other lemon half. You can drop the squeezed lemon halves right into the water too.

Cut each artichoke in half lengthwise and, using a teaspoon, remove and discard the hairy choke. Slice each cleaned artichoke lengthwise as thinly as possible using a mandoline or a very sharp chef's knife. Transfer the sliced artichokes to the bowl of water with lemon. The artichokes can be prepared up to this point 1 day in advance.

When you're ready to eat, pat the artichoke slices dry on paper towels and place them in a salad bowl. Dress them with a healthy pour of olive oil (3 or 4 tablespoons) and squeeze over the juice from the remaining lemon, discarding the seeds. Season the artichokes to taste with a healthy pinch of salt and scatter over the shaved cheese. Serve immediately.

Steamed Artichokes

The most understated dish in the world.

[SERVES 4]

4 large artichokes
Mayonnaise (page 264)

Using a pair of scissors, trim the sharp thorn from the tip of each leaf on each artichoke. Using a serrated knife, remove 2 inches from the crown. If needed, trim the stem back so each artichoke can balance in a serving bowl.

Place the artichokes in a steamer, cover, and cook until fork-tender, about 20 minutes. The artichokes may also be boiled in a large covered pot with ample salted water to cover them until done. Remove with a slotted spoon.

Serve the artichokes warm or chilled and enjoy with plenty of homemade mayonnaise. Dip each leaf into a bowl of the mayonnaise and scrape the flesh off the leaf with your teeth, creating a tall pile of spent leaves on a side plate as you go. When you reach the center of the artichoke, discard the fibrous choke and enjoy the incomparable heart. Remember to provide extra plates for the discarded leaves.

Fried Artichokes

Fried "in the Jewish style," these artichokes are said to have originated in the Jewish section of Rome. It's worth going to the trouble of thoroughly cleaning the artichokes as I've outlined below. This double-fry method, often employed in French fry making, ensures that you'll have artichokes that are both crispy on the outside and tender on the inside.

[SERVES 4]

8 small artichokes

Extra-virgin olive oil, for frying

Coarse salt

1 lemon, cut into wedges

Working with one artichoke at a time, hold on to the stem of the artichoke and remove the dark green outer leaves, one by one, to reveal the tender yellow leaves. Turn the artichoke around and, while holding on to the yellow leaves, use a potato peeler to clean away the tough, dark green skin from the stem. Using a teaspoon, dig down to remove the choke, found deep inside the flower between the leaves and at the base of the stem. Be careful not to scoop away the heart, just scratch the choke loose. Set the cleaned artichokes aside.

Heat 3 inches of olive oil in a deep, heavy pot over medium-low heat until it reaches 230°F on a candy thermometer, which is to say hot, but not terribly hot. To test the temperature without a thermometer, place one artichoke in the oil. Small bubbles should gently form around it. If the oil bubbles vigorously, reduce the heat. Place all of the cleaned artichokes into the oil and cook, stirring occasionally, until just tender and barely beginning to brown, about 10 minutes.

Using a slotted spoon, transfer the artichokes to a bowl, cover with plastic wrap, and let the artichokes cool to room temperature. This waiting period is crucial because the steam formed in the covered bowl will continue to cook the artichokes and guarantee that they're tender all the way through.

Meanwhile, turn the heat up under the oil until the temperature rises to 375°F. Return the artichokes to the pot and cook, turning a few times, until crisp and golden brown all over, about 4 minutes. Transfer the artichokes to a paper towel–lined plate, season with salt, and serve immediately with the lemon wedges.

Carciofi alla Romana

This classic Roman dish (braised artichokes) creates not only delicious, tender artichokes but also a gorgeous elixir of a broth. Good bread is essential when eating these so that you have something to sop up all of the incredible juice. These artichokes are as good cold as they are warm, so feel free to make them ahead, or for a party.

[SERVES 4]

4 garlic cloves, peeled

½ cup packed fresh mint leaves

6 high-quality anchovy fillets

8 medium artichokes

1 cup dry white wine

¼ cup extra-virgin olive oil

Coarse salt

Preheat the oven to 375°F.

Chop the garlic, mint, and anchovies together by hand or in a food processor until the mixture resembles a coarse pesto. Set the mixture aside.

Working with one artichoke at a time, hold on to the stem of the artichoke and remove and discard the dark green outer leaves, one by one, until only the tightly packed, pale green and yellow leaves are left. Then, holding each artichoke by the leaves, use a paring knife or a potato peeler to clean away the tough dark green skin from the stem. Trim off and discard the top inch or so of the artichoke and use a teaspoon to dig through the leaves and scoop out the thorny, bristly choke at the base of the vegetable. Be sure not to remove any of the beloved heart! Repeat the process with each artichoke.

In a baking dish or skillet large enough to hold all of the artichokes in a single layer, rub the mint mixture all over the artichokes. Pour the wine and olive oil over the artichokes and season generously with salt. Cover the dish or skillet with a lid or aluminum foil and place it in the oven. Roast, uncovering the dish to turn the artichokes every so often, until they are tender, about 1 hour. Serve warm or chilled, in the cooking juices.

Soupe au Pistou

I begin making this soup in spring as soon as basil arrives in the market, and the last bowl is served late into Indian summer. I allow the vegetables to change with the season and use leeks and favas in the spring instead of the green beans and zucchini of summer. Whatever vegetables you use, this soup is always made with water, and topped with an ample drizzle of extra-virgin olive oil and a generous spoonful of bright green basil *pistou*.

[SERVES 6 TO 8]

1 cup dried cannellini beans, soaked overnight and drained

1 cup dried cranberry beans, soaked overnight and drained

2 celery stalks, diced

2 large carrots, peeled and diced

1 medium yellow onion, peeled and diced

1 fennel bulb, including the light green stems, diced

One 15-ounce can whole peeled tomatoes, seeded and chopped

6 large outer escarole leaves, torn into pieces

1 large handful green beans, trimmed and cut in half crosswise

1 leek, white and light green parts only, thinly sliced

2 small zucchini, diced

Pinch red chili flakes, plus more as needed

Coarse salt

2 cups fresh basil leaves, washed and dried

½ cup extra-virgin olive oil, plus more for serving

½ cup grated Parmigiano-Reggiano cheese, plus more for serving

Place the soaked beans, all of the vegetables, the chili flakes, and 2 teaspoons of salt into a large soup pot and cover with cold water. Add 2 additional cups of water. Bring the mixture to a boil, lower the heat, and allow it to simmer until the beans are tender, about 1 hour, adding more water as the soup cooks if it gets too dry or too thick at any point. Season the soup to taste with additional salt and chili flakes, if necessary.

Meanwhile, place the basil leaves in a mortar and use a pestle to crush them with 2 teaspoons of salt. Work in the Parmigiano-Reggiano and the olive oil to make a coarse paste. Alternatively, you can pulse the basil, salt, and Parmigiano-Reggiano together in a food processor and stream in the olive oil to make the paste. Either way, season the pistou with additional salt, if necessary, and set it aside. A thin layer of olive oil poured on top will prevent the pistou from browning.

Serve the soup hot, topped with a generous drizzle of olive oil, a big spoonful of the pistou, and a handful of grated Parmigiano-Reggiano.

RECIPE NOTES

1. You can speed up the cooking by substituting two 15-ounce cans of beans for the dried beans. Simply rinse the beans under cold running water and drain them. Add them to the soup once the vegetables are tender and let the whole mixture cook for 15 minutes before serving.

2. Other uses for the more tender inner leaves of the escarole include Grilled Escarole (page 180), Poached Eggs over Scafata (page 13), or Fava Bean Salad (page 83).

Winter Legume Soup

This hearty soup is taken from the Sicilian tradition of emptying your cupboards at the end of winter to make a pot of soup and clear the way for spring. It's sometimes referred to as San Giuseppe Soup because spring-cleaning coincides with the celebration of Saint Joseph (*Giuseppe* in Italian). Note that the chickpeas must be soaked overnight, so plan ahead.

[MAKES A BIG POT; ENOUGH FOR AT LEAST 8 SERVINGS]

½ cup dried chickpeas

1 cup dried fava beans

1 cup green split peas

½ cup dried cranberry beans

½ cup green lentils

Extra-virgin olive oil

Leaves from 2 bunches Swiss chard, thoroughly washed and roughly chopped

1 yellow onion, peeled and finely diced

1 fennel bulb, trimmed and finely diced

1 tablespoon fennel seeds, finely ground

2 tablespoons Homemade Tomato Concentrate (page 266) or tomato paste

Freshly ground black pepper

Coarse salt

8 thick slices toast, rubbed with garlic, for serving

Place the chickpeas in a bowl, cover with cold water, and allow them to soak overnight. You can leave them out at room temperature or place them in the refrigerator. Wherever they're out of your way!

The next day, drain the chickpeas and set them aside.

Place the fava beans, split peas, cranberry beans, and lentils into a large bowl and cover with warm water. Let the legumes soak for half an hour. Drain them and set them aside, separate from the chickpeas.

Meanwhile, place ¼ cup of olive oil in a large soup pot over medium heat. Add the Swiss chard, onion, and fennel and cook, stirring occasionally, until the vegetables begin to soften, about 15 minutes.

Stir the ground fennel seeds and the tomato concentrate into the vegetables and cook until fragrant, just about a minute. Stir in the drained chickpeas and cover the mixture with water. Bring the soup to a boil, reduce the heat, and allow it to simmer for half an hour.

Add the reserved legumes to the pot and add enough water to cover. Cook until all of the legumes are tender and soft and the soup is quite thick, about 1½ hours, adding water as the soup is cooking if it gets too dry or too thick at any point. Season the soup with plenty of salt and pepper.

Place a piece of garlic-rubbed toast into the bottom of each of eight soup bowls, drizzle each slice liberally with olive oil, and season with salt and pepper. Ladle the hot soup over the toast and serve immediately.

RECIPE NOTE

Even though only the leaves from the Swiss chard should be used for this soup, don't discard the stems! Trim off any dark bits and cook the stems in salted, boiling water until just tender and then grill them with olive oil and salt and serve them just like that—especially good with fish. Or use the blanched stems to make a gratin, like the Cauliflower Gratin on page 181, but use Parmigiano-Reggiano cheese instead of Gruyère, and season the sauce with plenty of garlic.

PART 4.

JAMBON ET FROMAGE

Jambon et Fromage

Cheese and ham are the backbone of Buvette's menu. We have a curated selection
of each that we serve simply unadulterated with tall stacks of toast, and we also
tuck each of them into so many of Buvette's signature dishes. Our Croque-Monsieur
(page 69) would be nothing without the Gruyère cheese and prosciutto cotto ham
in between its béchamel-slicked layers. Tartiflette (page 182) and Aligot
(page 185) depend on their generous helpings of cheese to be memorable and so
often requested by our guests.

I really began to appreciate cheese when I worked at Caffé Arti e Mestieri in Reggio
Emilia in northern Italy. Often I would bicycle out to the countryside and visit
the artisans who supplied us with many of our products. One of the first of
many doors I knocked on was a small *caseificio*, a creamery, where they made
Parmigiano-Reggiano. The father-and-son team showed me how they made *grana*,
the Italian term for the Parmigiano-Reggiano, in their barn that housed a brilliant
copper kettle. The milk would coagulate in the kettle and turn into curds that
got passed through cheesecloth. After the curds were placed in weighted molds, the
excess moisture would be released, and the cheese took on its famous, drumlike
shape. After a bath in salted water, the cheese would age for exactly two years. The
technique had remained basically unchanged since the fourteenth century.

There is no better inspiration than being hands-on and knee-deep at the source,
watching one of your most beloved ingredients come to life. The barn air was
cool and smelled like cut grass and sweet cow dung. I can remember being distracted
by a half-dozen kittens playing under the table waiting for the excess fresh cheese
to be cut from the molds and thrown to the floor. Upstairs, the mother and daughter
fixed bowls of hot coffee with the creamery's fresh milk, which still had its thick cap
of cream—chunks floated on the surface and melted into pools of butter in the coffee, which we soaked up with torn pieces of day-old bread. More than just a fond
memory, the experience taught me that the more you know about the people who
make your favorite products, the more you enjoy them.

Baked Figs

Packed with the intoxicating combination of bay leaves, orange, almond, and sweet Banyuls wine, these figs come out of the oven infused with flavor, and their texture goes from quite dry to soft and jammy. As you eat these, be sure to discard the bay leaf from inside each fig, just as you would a pit from an olive. While these complement cheese beautifully, they can also be served for breakfast with yogurt or for dessert with crème fraîche or ice cream.

[SERVES 4]

A dozen dried figs

Zest of 1 orange, removed in large strips
with a vegetable peeler

6 fresh bay leaves

½ cup almonds

½ cup Banyuls or other sweet wine

Preheat the oven to 400°F.

Cut a small horizontal slit in each fig, being careful not to cut all the way through. Cut the orange zest into a dozen 1-inch-long pieces, and tear or cut each bay leaf in half. Stuff each fig with 1 piece of orange zest, half of a bay leaf, and 1 almond.

Pack the stuffed figs into a small baking dish that will hold them in a snug, even layer. Scatter over any additional almonds and any extra orange zest if you're left with some.

Pour the wine evenly over the figs, place another baking dish over the figs to weigh them down, and press firmly to really get the figs quite flat and saturated with the wine. Place the whole thing, including the second baking dish, into the oven and bake for 20 minutes.

Serve the figs hot, warm, or at room temperature, alongside just about any cheese.

Fruit in Parchment Paper

One of my favorite accompaniments for cheese is fruit *in cartoccio* (Italian) or *en papillotte* (French), which simply means "in paper." The packages are great to make ahead of time and are an unexpected alternative to the ubiquitous cluster of grapes that seem to accompany every cheese platter in the world. Feel free to vary the combination (diced pumpkin, apples, and dates are especially good) and the wine too. Vin santo could easily be Banyuls or Sauternes, even port. Serve the packages alongside dense bread and rich cheese, such as La Tur.

[SERVES 4]

2 tablespoons dried currants

½ cup vin santo

1 apple, peeled, cored, and thinly sliced

1 quince, peeled, cored, and thinly sliced

2 tablespoons honey

A pinch of coarse salt

¼ cup walnuts

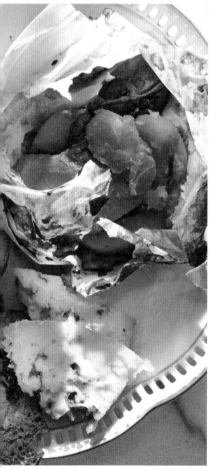

Preheat the oven to 450°F.

In a large bowl, soak the currants in the vin santo for at least 10 minutes. Once they're a bit softened, add the remaining ingredients and stir to combine.

Meanwhile, cut out four 8-inch squares of parchment paper. Evenly divide the mixture among the parchment squares. Bring the edges of each square together and fold them over each other, creating a continuous seal. Place the four packages on a baking sheet and roast in the oven until the fruit smells fragrant and the paper is browned, about 15 minutes.

Pesto di Parma

Waste not, want not! If you've lucked upon a whole leg of prosciutto and have worked through the whole thing and are faced with the end, *pesto di Parma* is for you. Of course you can also buy prosciutto ends; they're usually less expensive than prosciutto. To make pesto di Parma, dice the dry end of the prosciutto and pass it through a meat grinder, alternating it with equal amounts of chopped Parmigiano-Reggiano and adding a few fresh sage leaves per every handful of meat and cheese. Mix the ground mixture with extra-virgin olive oil, spread the coarse pesto on toast, and drizzle with *vincotto* (a sweet grape must).

RECIPE NOTE

A meat grinder is essential for this undertaking. A food processor, even if you just pulse it, will likely overprocess, and even overheat, the meat mixture, and because the meat is dry, it tends to get stuck on the blade. I know a meat grinder might sound like a big undertaking, but if you have a KitchenAid mixer, consider investing in the grinder attachment. Or buy an old-fashioned one, available at most kitchen stores and online too, which won't cost very much. Even if you don't make pesto di Parma often, you can grind your own beef, chicken, and even fish for all sorts of burgers, sausages, even kibbe, those Middle Eastern patties of beef or lamb mixed with bulgur, herbs, and spices. It's a worthwhile investment and a useful, old-fashioned tool.

The Language of Cheese

Just as there is for wine, there's a whole vocabulary for cheese. And, just like buying wine, the more you know, the more you value it. The most important thing to do when purchasing cheese is to taste it. Trust your instincts and buy what you like!

Some helpful terms:

1. **Cow** *in French is* vache *and in Italian it's* vacca *or* mucca.

2. *Sheep in French is* brebis *and in Italian it's* pecora.

3. *Goat in French is* chèvre *and in Italian it's* capra.

4. **Bloom** *refers to mold; not necessarily a bad thing.*

5. **Eyes** *refer to holes in the cheese. Swiss cheese, for example, has a lot of eyes.*

6. **Tears** *refers to the liquid that sometimes "weeps" from a cheese. Again, not necessarily a bad thing.*

7. **Rind** *refers to the outer surface of the cheese, which develops as the cheese ripens. It serves a tremendous purpose in that it keeps the cheese from drying out. The rind also contributes to the cheese's ultimate taste, especially a rind that has been washed with salted water or liquor. Even if they're a bit tough, most natural rinds are edible.*

8. *Adjectives used to describe cheese are very similar to the ones used to describe wine. For example: buttery, mellow, creamy, sharp, earthy, chalky, soapy, musty, tart, fruity, round, and smoky.*

How to Store Cheese

Wrap cheese tightly in waxed or parchment paper and then, if you'd like, place it in a plastic bag or container and keep it refrigerated. Bring to room temperature only the amount you are going to consume. After you've unwrapped a cheese, discard the paper. Always rewrap cheese in new paper to best preserve it.

How Much Cheese to Buy

To figure out how much cheese to buy for a party, know that 1 pound is 16 ounces, and that each guest will usually consume about 3 ounces of cheese.

Buvette / The Pleasure of Good Food

Thoughts on Nuts and Their Shells

I frequently place baskets of nuts and nutcrackers on each table as a sign of hospitality. The guests are encouraged to help themselves and feel free to make a mess. (And I get to use my vintage table butler for cleanup—now that is service!)

A Little Advice on Hams

I have eaten my share of cured pork and then some. I spent a considerable amount of time in the hills neighboring Parma where Italian prosciutto is perfected. I have also enjoyed cured hams from Spain, France, and Virginia—all exquisite hams with subtle differences in breed, cure time, and diet.

It is all about the flavor, or in another word, the fat. Cured pork is an ancient equation of time, salt, and diet. Prosciutto di Parma has a long history reaching back to Roman times. The hindquarters of large white pigs are treated with salt and cured in mountain air for up to twenty-four months. I remember visiting the hills near Parma where thousands of pork legs would be curing overhead in the mountain air. The barns have large open windows on all sides for cross ventilation. Prosciutto di Parma is noted for having a layer of fat, at least two fingers deep, that holds a lot of flavor.

Spanish Ibérico de Bellota is another exquisite cured ham, always made from the smaller black Iberian breed, which are fed a diet of only acorns. The pork is lightly salted and left to cure, usually up to twenty-four months. It is drier and saltier resulting in a deep red meat color and a concentration of flavor in the fat.

The French cured ham is known as Jambon de Bayonne. It is aged a little less, usually seven to ten months, and cured in salt as well. All three hams are classic variations of the same, but American cured hams, usually associated with the South, are salt-cured and often smoked. S. Wallace Edwards ham from Virginia is one of the best smoked country hams, which can be eaten hand sliced just like prosciutto.

PART 5

APÉRITIFS

Apéritifs

L'heure de l'apéro is a local tradition in France as well as the States. We call it happy hour, the most relaxing part of the day. When your day is done and you look forward to a pleasurable meal, you will find *l'apéritif* a refreshing interlude.

Venice, Italy, is one of my favorite places to enjoy an *aperitivo* whether I am standing at the workingman's Scavone, or seated at the bar in the elegant Gritti Palace on the Grand Canal. Both are equally delicious and delightful. The bar at the Gritti is only four feet long, but I consider it the cocktail altar. I worshiped each evening with a negroni. I was presented with *salatini*, little salty snacks, like cheesy *gougères*, savory chicken liver toasts, and generous bowls of macadamia nuts. I appreciated the detail it took to serve a simple Campari and soda, from silver trays to folded napkins. *Aperitivo* translates to "appetite stimulant," and even though the snacks were intended as a prelude to dinner, we'd make a meal out of them and toast our handsome drinks.

To this day, the feeling I had there—a combination of feeling taken care of, of the atmosphere being so warm that it's easy to connect with whomever you're with, of feeling like simple things can be terrifically special—is what I try to re-create every evening at Buvette.

During the interim long after lunch, but just before dinner, when the day needs its edge taken off and you're beginning to get hungry, a cocktail and a small amount of food is in order. The following pages include not only my favorite drinks, but also ideas and advice for setting up a bar and recipes for my most beloved "bar snacks," including homemade potato chips, all sorts of *tartinettes* using easy walnut pesto, and classic charcuterie like country-style pâté that can be made ahead and served on toast alongside a bowl of cornichons. Cheers!

A FEW APÉRITIF MENUS

A SPRINGTIME LUNCHEON

Lillet on Ice with
Orange Slices

Kir Royales

Breakfast Radishes
with Bagna Cauda

Salmon Rillettes with
Horseradish on Toast

Walnut Pesto Tartinettes

A BACHELOR PARTY

Perfect Martinis and
Classic Manhattans

Ciambottini

Oxtail Marmalade
Tartinettes

Brandade de Morue
on Toast

Apple and Cheese Fricos

NEW YEAR'S EVE APÉRITIFS

Champagne

Potato Chips with
Rosemary Salt

Marinated Olives with
Orange Zest and Red Chili

Gougères with Gruyère,
Mustard, and Rosemary

Breakfast Radishes with Bagna Cauda

I used to sit at the counter between lunch and dinner service when I lived in Italy, and turn the pages of old cookbooks, coveting all of the traditional dishes. *Bagna cauda,* or "warm bath," is a classic preparation of three prized ingredients: olive oil, garlic, and anchovies. While it's great for any crunchy vegetable, including sliced fennel and scallions, the most classic accompaniment is spicy radishes. I like thin, white-tipped French breakfast radishes for this, but normal ones are perfect too.

[MAKES ½ CUP BAGNA CAUDA; ENOUGH FOR RADISHES FOR 4 PEOPLE]

1 large bunch breakfast radishes,
cut in half lengthwise

6 garlic cloves, crushed (don't
even bother to peel them)

A dozen high-quality,
fat anchovy fillets

½ teaspoon coarse salt

½ cup extra-virgin olive oil

Place the radishes in ice-cold water while you prepare the bagna cauda. This will help them be as crisp as possible.

Meanwhile, place the garlic, anchovies, salt, and olive oil in a small saucepan over low heat and cook, stirring every so often, until the anchovies have dissolved into the oil and the garlic is a little bit softened, about 10 minutes. Be sure to keep the heat low enough that the garlic does not threaten to burn. Remove the bagna cauda from the heat.

Drain and dry the radishes and serve drizzled generously with the bagna cauda.

> RECIPE NOTE
> Leave a bit of the stem on the radishes so that they not only look appealing but also offer your guests something to hold on to while eating.

Ciambottini

Full disclosure: I made this word up. Like cooking, my language skills are homegrown. I turned *ciambotta*, which means "big mix," into a longer word with a smaller meaning: *"ciambottini"* is a little mix. For me, it's a vinegary, salty, can't-get-enough combination of artichokes, bite-size pieces of pecorino cheese, soppressata, and briny caperberries. Ciambottini is a strong cocktail's best friend.

[SERVES 4]

½ cauliflower, cut into bite-size florets

3 small preserved artichokes, quartered lengthwise

3 ounces pecorino Romano, cut into 1-inch pieces

3 ounces hard salami, cut into bite-size pieces

2 tablespoons large caperberries

½ cup mixed green and black olives

1 or 2 dried red chilies or a large pinch of red chilies

1 cup extra-virgin olive oil

3 tablespoons sherry or red wine vinegar

1 roasted red bell pepper, skinned, stemmed, and seeded, cut into large strips

4 bay leaves

Bring a large pot of water to a boil and add the cauliflower. Cook until just tender, about 2 minutes. Drain the cauliflower and let it cool to room temperature.

Place the cauliflower in a large bowl and thoroughly mix it together with all of the remaining ingredients. Serve the ciambottini at room temperature.

Gougères with Gruyère, Mustard, and Rosemary

Warm, salty, and irresistible, *gougères* elevate whatever moment they are served in. Mine are so densely packed with cheese that just after they heroically attempt to rise in the hot oven, all they can muster is deflating. In my eyes, this is a good thing. You can get a puffy, crispy gougère anywhere—but those are always empty inside. A gougère so flavorful that it falls flat on its face? That's my kind of gougère.

[MAKES 2 DOZEN GOUGÈRES]

9 tablespoons (1 stick plus 1 tablespoon) unsalted butter

2 shallots, peeled and finely diced

2 teaspoons finely chopped fresh rosemary

1¼ cups water

1 teaspoon coarse salt

1 cup unbleached all-purpose flour

5 large eggs

1½ cups grated Gruyère cheese (about 5 ounces), plus a little extra for the tops

½ teaspoon freshly ground black pepper

Pinch cayenne pepper

2 tablespoons Dijon mustard

Preheat the oven to 425°F. Line two baking sheets with parchment paper.

Heat 1 tablespoon of the butter in a small skillet over medium-high heat. Add the shallots and rosemary to the pan and cook, stirring a bit, just until softened, 2 to 3 minutes. Remove the skillet from the heat and set it aside.

Meanwhile, combine the remaining 8 tablespoons butter with the water and salt in a small saucepan and bring to a boil. Add the flour all at once, reduce the heat to medium, and stir vigorously until the mixture forms a dough that begins to pull away from the sides of the pot and doesn't stick to the sides or bottom, a good 5 or 6 minutes. It should be quite shiny and smell buttery and wonderful.

Transfer the dough to the bowl of a stand mixer fitted with the whisk attachment and beat until the dough has cooled off a bit, about 5 minutes. Alternatively, you can do this with a handheld electric mixer or just a whisk and some serious forearm muscle.

Crack the eggs, one by one, into a small bowl and add them to the dough, waiting until each one is incorporated before adding the next. Keep mixing the dough until it comes together. (It will separate a bit each time you add an egg, but don't despair, it will find its way back to itself.)

Once the dough has formed, add the reserved shallot mixture, the Gruyère, black pepper, cayenne, and mustard and mix just to combine. Using two spoons, place golf ball–size dollops of the dough on the prepared baking sheets, leaving 2 inches between each. Sprinkle the top of each gougère with a pinch of extra grated Gruyère (you could also use Parmigiano-Reggiano for this).

Bake, rotating the baking sheets halfway through baking, so that the gougères cook evenly, until they're a bit puffed and very nicely browned, about 20 minutes. Serve while hot.

> **RECIPE NOTE**
> If you don't bake these right away, portion them on a parchment paper–lined baking sheet and freeze them. When frozen, place them in an airtight container and store them in the freezer for up to 2 months. Bake them without thawing, allowing a few extra minutes in the oven.

Rosemary Potato Chips

I can't imagine a more desired food than a potato chip. As the saying goes, "you can't have just one." I like to serve potato chips in silver bowls or even on silver pedestals, noting the extraordinary potential of one of the most ordinary of foods. Keep in mind that the potatoes must soak for at least 20 minutes before frying, but they can sit that way for up to a day, so do slice them ahead of time and plan ahead.

[SERVES 4]

1 teaspoon very finely chopped fresh rosemary leaves

1 teaspoon coarse salt

2 russet potatoes, peeled

Oil, for frying (corn, peanut, vegetable, canola, or grapeseed oil all work well)

In a small bowl, stir together the rosemary and the salt and set aside.

Using a mandoline or a very sharp knife, carefully slice the potatoes into thin rounds no more than ⅛ inch thick. Place the sliced potatoes into a bowl of cold water and let them sit for at least 20 minutes so that they release some of their starch. You can let them sit in the water in the refrigerator up to a few hours, even overnight, if you'd like to plan ahead.

Drain the potatoes and dry them thoroughly on paper towels.

Pour enough oil into a large, heavy pot so that you have at least 2 to 3 inches of oil, but make sure the oil does not fill the pot more than halfway. Set the pot over high heat and let it heat until the oil reaches 350°F on a candy thermometer. If you don't have a thermometer, place 1 slice of potato into the oil and when bubbles form around it and it is really sizzling, you will know that your oil is hot enough for frying.

Carefully add a few handfuls of your dry potatoes to the oil, being careful not to crowd the pot. Fry the chips, stirring occasionally with a wooden or slotted spoon, until the potatoes are browned and crisp, about 4 minutes. Using a slotted spoon, carefully transfer the potatoes to a paper towel–lined plate to drain while you continue frying the potato slices in batches.

Once all of the chips are fried, sprinkle them with the reserved rosemary salt and serve immediately, ideally with a strong cocktail.

Marinated Olives with Orange Zest and Red Chili

Feel free to use this recipe as a guide, changing the type of olives and seasonings as you please. For example, try crushed fennel seeds and lemon on bright green olives, or a combination of coriander and cumin seeds on oil-cured, black Moroccan olives. These can be made ahead and rewarmed just before serving, or simply served at room temperature.

[MAKES 2 CUPS MARINATED OLIVES]

1 cup green olives, rinsed and drained

1 cup black olives, rinsed and drained

¼ cup extra-virgin olive oil

1 tablespoon Herbes de Provence (page 261)

Zest of 1 orange, removed in large strips with a vegetable peeler

2 dried red chilies, or a pinch of red chili flakes

Place all of the ingredients in a skillet and stir to combine. Set the skillet over medium heat and cook until the olives are warmed through and the aromatics are fragrant, 4 to 5 minutes. Remove the pan from the heat and serve the olives warm, or let them cool and serve at room temperature.

Apple and Cheese Fricos

You know the little bits of cheese that stick to the pan when you make a grilled cheese sandwich? The ones that get crispy and brown and that you can't help but scrape up and eat when no one is looking? A *frico* is a larger portion of that perfect bite. Though it's sometimes made with Parmigiano-Reggiano cheese, I use Montasio, a cow's-milk cheese from Friuli, where the frico originated. The apples here aren't totally traditional, but are quite nice.

[MAKES 4 FRICOS]

Extra-virgin olive oil

1½ cups coarsely grated Montasio cheese
(or other aged cow's-milk cheese)

1 Gala apple, stemmed, cored,
and thinly sliced

4 fresh sage leaves

Set a heavy medium skillet over medium heat and pour in enough olive oil to thinly coat the entire surface of the pan. Sprinkle a quarter of the cheese evenly over the surface of the pan and scatter over a quarter of the apple slices and a sage leaf. Cook until the cheese has completely melted, is bubbling, and is golden brown on its underside. Using a spatula, carefully fold half the cheese over to form a half-moon shape (like an omelette) and transfer the frico to a square of parchment paper. Continue to make fricos with the remaining cheese and apples, adding more oil to the pan as necessary. Serve warm.

Tartinettes and Crostini

All over France you find tartines or in Italy you find crostini—both are wonderful open-faced sandwiches. At Buvette, I serve tartinettes, which are smaller versions of the same. A vehicle for just about anything, tartinettes or crostini invite improvisation. They are a miraculous way to use up all sorts of leftover bits of cheese, pickled vegetables, meats, pestos, and more. They can be sweet—say, ricotta and good honey or roasted fruit—and can be served for breakfast, lunch, dinner, or with drinks. They are my most favorite way of taking a dish I love and reducing it down to a single bite—oxtail marmalade, for example. Below you'll find three of my favorites to have alongside a cocktail or glass of wine, a promise of the meal to come.

BUTTER AND ANCHOVY TARTINETTES

[MAKES 6 TARTINETTES]

8 tablespoons (1 stick) highest-quality, unsalted butter, preferably cultured, at room temperature

8 small pieces toasted country bread

Coarse salt

12 salt-packed anchovies, rinsed and dried

8 large caperberries

Place the butter in the bowl of a stand mixer fitted with the paddle attachment and beat until light and airy. Alternatively, place the butter in a bowl and beat with a whisk and a lot of elbow grease until light and airy.

Spread a thick layer of the butter on a slice of toast, sprinkle it with flaky salt, lay over one or two of the rinsed and dried anchovies, and top off each one with a caperberry.

WALNUT PESTO TARTINETTES

Use this nutty pesto as a thick spread on crunchy grilled toast. Food critic Frank Bruni called this pesto "adult peanut butter" in a *New York Times* review. That was a compliment, I think.

[MAKES 1 CUP PESTO; ENOUGH FOR 6 TARTINETTES]

1 cup raw walnut halves

1½ ounces Parmigiano-Reggiano cheese, coarsely grated (about ¼ cup packed)

1 small garlic clove, roughly chopped

2 teaspoons fresh thyme leaves

1 teaspoon sherry vinegar

¼ cup plus 2 tablespoons extra-virgin olive oil

2 tablespoons finely chopped sun-dried tomatoes (either packed in oil or softened in hot water for 10 minutes; either way, be sure to drain them)

Coarse salt

A few slices country bread, grilled or toasted

In a food processor, pulse the walnuts, cheese, garlic, and thyme with the sherry vinegar until coarsely chopped. Transfer the mixture to a bowl and stir in the olive oil and tomatoes. Season with salt and serve with toasted bread. The pesto will keep, covered, in the refrigerator for up to a week.

POMODORINI CROSTINI

This flavorful Mediterranean combination—dried tomatoes and capers—makes a piquant marriage with stracchino cheese or any other soft, creamy cow's-milk cheese, even scrambled eggs.

[MAKES 1 CUP POMODORINI; ENOUGH FOR 6 CROSTINI]

1 cup sun-dried cherry tomatoes (about 2 ounces)

2 tablespoons capers

½ teaspoon dried wild oregano

1 small garlic clove, finely minced

2 teaspoons sherry vinegar

¼ cup extra-virgin olive oil

Pinch coarse salt

A few slices country bread, grilled or toasted

Stracchino cheese, for serving

Place the tomatoes in a small bowl, cover with very hot water, and let them soak until they're soft, about 1 hour. Drain the tomatoes, roughly chop them, and combine them with the rest of the ingredients. Serve immediately on grilled bread with a bit of soft cheese, preferably stracchino. The spread keeps, covered with a thin layer of olive oil, in an airtight container in the refrigerator for up to a week.

Favorite Topping Combinations for Morning Tartinettes

1. Mascarpone cheese, sweetened with honey and topped with blackberries and/or raspberries that have been mixed with orange juice and zest and a bit more honey. Very nice topped with bee pollen.

2. Almond butter, drizzled with maple syrup, sprinkled with salt, and topped with sliced fresh figs.

3. Farmers' cheese topped with flaked smoked trout and thinly sliced scallions.

4. Quark and dried cherries that have been poached in water and sugar.

5. Farmers' cheese with thinly sliced smoked salmon and pickled red onions.

Oxtail Marmalade

Remember, big dishes can be small dishes. This deeply concentrated version of braised oxtails is a lot of heft in a small package. Not only can you make this in advance, but it's actually better if you do. Oxtails can be purchased in most grocery stores, or from ethnic or specialty butchers.

[MAKES 3 CUPS; ENOUGH FOR 6 TO 8 PEOPLE AS AN APPETIZER]

3 pounds oxtails, cut into 2-inch pieces

Coarse salt

Freshly ground black pepper

3 tablespoons extra-virgin olive oil

1 yellow onion, peeled and diced

1 large carrot, peeled and diced

1 large celery stalk, diced

2 garlic cloves, peeled and minced

2 cups white wine

3 ounces bittersweet chocolate, roughly chopped

1 bay leaf

4 juniper berries, crushed

Two 5-inch sprigs fresh rosemary

Zest of ½ orange, removed in large strips with a vegetable peeler

1 cup water

1 tablespoon sherry vinegar

1 tablespoon honey

¼ cup golden raisins

¼ cup raw walnuts, chopped

Warm toast, for serving

Preheat the oven to 350°F.

Season the oxtail pieces aggressively with salt and pepper on all sides. Heat the olive oil in a large, heavy pot over medium-high heat and sear the oxtails until browned all over, about 5 minutes a side. Transfer the browned oxtails to a plate. Remove and discard all but 2 tablespoons of fat from the pot.

Add the onion, carrot, celery, and garlic to the remaining fat in the pot and cook, stirring now and again, until the vegetables are just beginning to soften, about 10 minutes. Add the white wine to the pot, increase the heat to high, and bring the mixture to a boil. Cook until the wine has reduced slightly, about 5 minutes. Stir in the chocolate, bay leaf, juniper, rosemary, orange zest, and water to the pot and return the browned oxtails to the mixture.

Cover the pot, transfer to the oven, and braise until the meat is incredibly tender, about 2½ hours.

Remove the oxtails from the oven and set aside to cool. When cool enough to handle, remove all of the meat from the bones and set it aside on a plate. Discard the bones as well as the rosemary sprigs, bay leaf, and strips of orange zest.

Set the pot with the cooking liquid and vegetables over high heat and bring it to a boil. Cook until the mixture is wonderfully thick and reduced, about 10 minutes. Turn off the heat and stir in the reserved oxtail meat, the vinegar, honey, raisins, and walnuts. Season the mixture with salt and pepper. Serve warm on toast.

A NOTE ON WINE
Serve this with a big, bold red wine from Piedmont's Monferrato region.

On Including Unusual Items on My Menu
I make a point of offering dishes like tripe, kidneys, and even cuttlefish and peas prepared the old Italian way by cooking them for hours. I know that not everyone is going to order these dishes, but for me it is worth it for the two or three people who might. I love those customers.

Duck Confit

Cooked and preserved in its own fat, duck confit is one of the most elegant examples of the intersection of decadence, simplicity, and economy. It's an essential component of Cassoulet (page 204) and also makes a wonderful meal. It is especially good alongside a hearty side dish like Lentils with Kale and Shallots (page 176) or Radicchio with Pine Nuts, Currants, and Aged Balsamic (page 168).

[MAKES 2 DUCK LEGS; EASILY MULTIPLIED]

3 tablespoons coarse salt

2 teaspoons very finely chopped fresh rosemary

2 teaspoons coarsely ground fennel seeds

2 duck legs (thigh attached)

1 cup duck fat or extra-virgin olive oil

3 garlic cloves (no need to even peel them)

2 shallots (no need to even peel them)

In a small bowl, stir together the salt, rosemary, and fennel seeds. Rub the mixture all over the duck legs, place them in a sealable plastic bag, and refrigerate overnight.

Preheat the oven to 325°F. Remove the duck legs from the bag and brush off the salt mixture.

Place the duck legs, fat, garlic, and shallots into a large, heavy pot or roasting pan. Cover tightly with a lid or aluminum foil and roast in the oven until the meat is tender and the fat has significantly rendered, about 2 hours. Let the duck cool to room temperature. It can sit, covered in all that fat, in the refrigerator for up to a month.

When you're ready to eat the duck, remove it from the fat and either broil it on a rack set on a sheet pan until the skin is crisp, or brown and crisp it in a pan on the stovetop. You can also remove the skin from the duck confit, take the meat off of the bone, discard the bones, and warm the meat in a pan or in the oven before serving.

TURNING DUCK CONFIT INTO DUCK RILLETTES

Break all of the meat and skin off the bones and discard the bones. Very finely (like, extremely finely) chop the meat and the skin. Mash in the garlic and shallots that were softened during the confit, being sure to discard their skins. Add a healthy pinch of Pâté Spice (page 261) and saturate the meat with warm duck fat. Keep stirring the mixture as it cools so that everything is evenly emulsified. As it cools,

the duck fat will solidify and the duck will become wonderfully thick and spreadable. Pack the mixture into small ramekins or into a large crock. Pour a little duck fat over the top to seal the rillettes. Store the rillettes in the refrigerator for up to a couple of weeks. Serve with toasted country bread and some cornichons and olives.

RECIPE NOTE

On Duck Fat

An abundance of duck fat is pretty much the best part of duck confit. Keep it in a closed container in your refrigerator and, most important, keep it accessible. Some of my favorite uses for duck fat include frying Potato Pancakes (page 184), roasting potatoes, or frying eggs.

Chicken Liver Mousse

A mousse is a delicate thing and, while it's easy to prepare, you must pay careful attention to it to avoid overcooking. Preparing the mousse in individual ramekins makes serving incredibly easy. To make it ahead of time, top the chilled mousse with a thin layer of aspic or clarified butter, which will keep air out and add flavor too. Serve with toasted Fruit Focaccia (page 73) or toasted country bread.

[SERVES 4]

2 tablespoons unsalted butter, plus extra for coating the ramekins

1 small shallot, minced

1 large garlic clove, finely minced or puréed on a Microplane grater

¼ cup Pineau des Charentes (a fortified French wine) or Banyuls

¼ pound chicken livers, large veins removed and discarded, rinsed and dried

¾ cup heavy cream

1 large egg

1½ teaspoons coarse salt

½ teaspoon freshly ground white pepper

Pinch cayenne pepper

½ teaspoon freshly grated nutmeg

Pinch ground cloves

Melted Clarified Butter (page 265) or Aspic (see opposite; optional)

Toasted brioche, cornichons, and olives, for serving

Preheat the oven to 325°F. Set a kettle of water on to boil. Butter four 6-ounce ramekins and set them aside.

Melt the butter in a small skillet over medium heat. Add the shallot and the garlic and cook, stirring a bit, until the vegetables soften, about 5 minutes. Add the Pineau and bring the mixture to a boil. Let it cook until the alcohol burns off, just under a minute, then remove the pan from the heat and allow the mixture to cool.

Transfer the mixture to a blender and add the chicken livers, cream, egg, salt, and spices. Purée the mixture until completely smooth and then pass it through a fine-mesh sieve into a clean pitcher or bowl. Evenly divide the mixture among the prepared ramekins, filling each about two-thirds full.

Place the ramekins in a large baking dish and transfer it to the oven. Pull the rack out a little bit and carefully pour hot water into the baking dish so that it comes halfway up the sides of the ramekins. Gently close the oven door to avoid splashing hot water into the mousse.

Bake until each mousse is set and the tip of a knife comes out clean when you insert it, about 35 minutes. Carefully remove the baking dish from the oven and remove the ramekins, using either tongs or oven mitts. Let them cool to room temperature.

When cool, cover with a thin layer of the melted clarified butter or aspic, if using. Set the ramekins in the refrigerator and let them cool for at least 2 hours before serving. They can be made up to 2 or 3 days in advance.

Serve cold with toast and a handful of cornichons and olives, if you'd like. Or use the mousse to make an elegant "adult PB&J" by spreading it on toasted brioche with a slick of Homemade Tomato Concentrate (page 266).

ASPIC

2 teaspoons powdered gelatin

½ cup cold water

¼ cup Pineau des Charentes or Banyuls

Pinch sugar

Pinch coarse salt

Place the gelatin into a bowl with the cold water and stir to combine. Meanwhile, place the Pineau in a saucepan with the sugar and salt and bring to a boil. Pour the hot Pineau over the gelatin and stir to combine. Let the mixture sit for 10 minutes before spooning it over the Chicken Liver Mousse, if desired, then allow it to set completely in the refrigerator.

Salmon Rillettes with Horseradish

This recipe is an adaptation of Thomas Keller's famous version. I first learned how to make it when I worked for him at Rakel, his long-gone restaurant that was on Varick Street in downtown Manhattan. It is possible to make this recipe in the amount of time it takes to chill a bottle of Champagne, which, incidentally, is a perfect pairing.

[SERVES 4]

¼ pound center-cut wild salmon

1 tablespoon extra-virgin olive oil

Coarse salt

4 tablespoons (½ stick) unsalted butter, at room temperature

1 small shallot, peeled and finely diced

1 tablespoon freshly grated horseradish or drained Pickled Horseradish (page 263)

1 small garlic clove, finely minced or puréed on a Microplane grater

¼ cup crème fraîche

¼ pound smoked salmon, finely diced

1 tablespoon freshly squeezed lemon juice

Freshly ground white pepper

Melted Clarified Butter (page 265) (optional)

Leafy greens and grilled toast, for serving

Prepare a steamer for cooking. If you do not have a steamer, fill a large pot with an inch of water, place a small bowl in the center of the pot, and rest a dinner plate on top of the bowl. Bring the water to a boil and, voilà, you've got a steamer!

Meanwhile, remove and discard the pin bones, skin, and all the dark connective tissue from the salmon. Rub the salmon with the olive oil and season liberally with salt. Place the salmon in the steamer, or on your plate-as-steamer, cover, and cook until it's just barely cooked through, 6 to 8 minutes. Transfer the salmon to a plate to cool down; it will continue to cook as it cools.

Meanwhile, heat 1 tablespoon of the butter in a small skillet over medium heat. Add the shallot, horseradish, and garlic and cook, stirring occasionally, until the vegetables soften, about 5 minutes. Set them aside to cool.

Put the remaining 3 tablespoons butter in a bowl and whip it with a whisk until it's creamy. Beat the crème fraîche and the shallot mixture into the butter. Fold in the diced smoked salmon. Gently break the cooked salmon apart and fold it into the mix. Add the lemon juice and season the mixture with salt and white pepper.

The rillettes are now ready to be served, or they can be packed into crocks, topped with clarified butter, covered, and stored in the refrigerator for up to 3 days. Serve at room temperature with leafy greens and grilled toast.

Pâté de Campagne

This country pâté is the keystone to any charcuterie repertoire. A thick slice of this classic terrine makes a nice lunch alongside leafy greens or a first course for a casual Sunday supper. Dressed up with sliced black truffles, it's ready for a holiday feast. The shopping list is the most intimidating part of the recipe, but the technique, no different than making meatloaf, is pretty straightforward. The terrine needs to rest overnight, so plan ahead.

[MAKES ONE 1-QUART TERRINE; ENOUGH FOR 12 PORTIONS]

½ pound sliced bacon

¼ pound slab bacon

¼ pound fresh pork fatback

1 pound pork shoulder

¼ pound pork or chicken livers

2 tablespoons extra-virgin olive oil

1 shallot, peeled and finely diced

3 garlic cloves, finely minced or puréed on a Microplane grater

½ small yellow onion, peeled and finely diced

½ cup dry white wine

2 cups homemade, fresh bread crumbs (page 268)

¼ cup Pineau des Charentes (a fortified French wine), sherry, or cognac

2 tablespoons finely chopped fresh flat-leaf parsley

3½ teaspoons coarse salt

1 teaspoon Pâté Spice (page 261)

½ teaspoon dried thyme

½ teaspoon dried marjoram

½ teaspoon dried tarragon

Pinch ground allspice

1 teaspoon freshly ground black pepper

¼ cup shelled pistachios

1 large egg, beaten

Toast, whole-grain mustard, and cornichons, for serving

Line a 1-quart, rectangular terrine mold with the sliced bacon, being sure to let the ends of the bacon hang over the edge. Place the prepared mold in the refrigerator while you prepare the pâté.

Cut the slab bacon, pork fatback, and pork shoulder into a fine dice. Chop the livers until they seem almost puréed. Run your knife through the meats and livers together to achieve a finer blend. There's no need for a grinder or fancy tools here, as the most delicious terrines are chopped by hand. Place the chopped meats into a bowl and set aside in the refrigerator.

Warm the olive oil in a large skillet over medium heat. Add the shallot, garlic, and onion and cook, stirring occasionally, until softened and translucent, about 10 minutes. Add the white wine and bring the mixture to a boil. »CONTINUES

Cook until the wine has reduced by half, about 5 minutes. Set the mixture aside to cool.

In a large bowl, stir together the bread crumbs and the fortified wine. Add the cooled vegetables along with the remaining ingredients and stir vigorously with a wooden spoon to make sure everything is combined thoroughly. Combine this mixture with the reserved meat mixture. For optimal flavor, cover the final pâté mixture with plastic wrap and allow it to sit in the refrigerator overnight for the flavors to meld.

Meanwhile, preheat the oven to 325°F. Set a kettle of water on to boil.

Evenly pack the pâté mixture into the prepared mold. Wrap the ends of the bacon over the pâté and place the lid of the terrine on top. If your terrine mold does not have a lid, wrap it tightly with aluminum foil. Place the terrine in a large baking dish and set it in the oven. Pull the rack out a little bit and carefully pour hot water into the baking dish so that it comes about two-thirds of the way up the sides of the terrine. Gently close the oven door to avoid splashing hot water into the mousse.

Bake until a thermometer inserted into the terrine registers 145°F, or until it's firm to the touch, about 2 hours. Carefully remove the terrine from the oven and out of the baking dish. Place the entire terrine on a sheet pan. Remove the lid and place a piece of parchment paper over the surface of the pâté. Press down on the parchment paper with something heavy (a wine bottle works) so that the terrine gets nice and flat and even. The juice will come out of the pâté when you press it down—that's what the sheet pan is for. Baste the pâté with these juices as it cools down to room temperature.

Once the pâté has cooled, remove it from the terrine mold and wrap it well in plastic wrap. Refrigerate it overnight before slicing.

Serve cold or at room temperature with plenty of toast, whole-grain mustard, and cornichons.

Aperitifs and Cocktails

Cocktails should be like clothing: change them depending on the season. In the heat of summer, nothing is better than a glass of cold Lillet served with tons of ice and a slice each of lemon and orange. A classic Manhattan made of strong bourbon braced with bitters and vermouth warms you in winter. A martini, like a pair of jeans, is good year-round. Keep in mind that cocktails are as much about the quality of your ingredients as they are about ceremony. Even the simplest drinks, which are my favorite drinks, require attention and care to make properly. Choose a beautiful glass, take the time to measure the correct ratios, use fresh ice, and don't drink too quickly.

AMAROS (ITALIAN HERBAL LIQUEURS, OFTEN BITTER)

Campari: My favorite first drink of the evening is a classic Campari (about an ounce) topped with soda (about 2 ounces) with a nice big slice of orange, served over ice.

Cynar: An artichoke bitter digestif, it is usually drunk on the rocks with soda.

Aperol: Made from rhubarb, Aperol is an *amaro* that is customarily served with a splash of orange juice and white wine.

LILLET

This classic French aperitif made of wine, citrus liqueurs, and quinine (what makes tonic taste like tonic) is available in white (*blanc*), red, and rosé varieties. Whichever you choose, chill the bottle well and pour it over plenty of ice with a slice of lemon and a slice of orange in each wineglass or rocks glass.

PERNOD

Pernod is a French liqueur that tastes like anise. It's used more often for cooking (with mussels, for example) than for drinking, but it does make a nice aperitif. To serve Pernod, place the bottle right on the table along with a tray filled with glasses, a pitcher of water, and a bowl of ice and let your guests mix drinks as they like them. In old French cafés, waiters used to splash a bit of Pernod on their towels and wipe down the table to perfume the air.

THREE SPARKLING WINE COCKTAILS

1. **Framboise:** A splash of raspberry liqueur topped with prosecco

2. **Classique:** Champagne poured over a spoonful of sugar that has been doused with bitters

3. **Rosette:** Amarena cherries topped with prosecco

KIR

For a kir, pour an ounce of crème de cassis (black currant liqueur) into a wineglass and top with cold white wine. For a kir royale, replace the wineglass with a Champagne flute and the white wine with Champagne. For a Communard, combine the cassis with red wine.

A PERFECT MARTINI

Chill a martini glass. Place a splash of vermouth into a mixing glass. Swirl it around so that the entire glass is coated with a whisper of vermouth. If you like your martini quite dry, pour out whatever vermouth is left in the mixing glass (otherwise, leave it in). Fill the mixing glass with ice. Don't skimp on this step—ice is necessary to effectively chill and blend the other ingredients. Place 3 ounces of gin or vodka into the mixing glass. Stir for 30 seconds and then strain the mixture into the chilled martini glass. Garnish with olives, if you'd like, and serve immediately.

A GOOD NEGRONI

Stir equal parts Campari, gin, and Carpano Antica sweet vermouth (1 to 1¼ ounces of each, or just shy of a shot of each) with ice and serve on the rocks with a slice of orange.

A CLASSIC MANHATTAN

Chill your tumbler and drop an Amarena cherry into it. Rub a piece of orange peel over the inside of the glass and leave it in the glass. Fill your mixing glass with ice and pour over 1 ounce of sweet vermouth, 3 ounces of bourbon, and 3 to 5 dashes of bitters. Stir until well chilled and the ice begins to loosen. Strain into the seasoned, cold glass and serve immediately.

PIMM'S CUP

Fill a glass with ice and pour over half Pimm's (an herbal British liqueur) and half Old-Fashioned Lemonade (page 94). Fill the drink with sliced lemons, oranges, apples, cucumber, strawberries, and mint.

BEE'S KNEES

For one drink, place 1½ ounces of gin in a cocktail shaker over plenty of ice and add 1 teaspoon of honey and 1 teaspoon of freshly squeezed lemon juice. Cover the shaker and shake vigorously. Strain the drink into a coupe and serve immediately.

A Bar at Home

May I suggest to you that a bar is a state of mind more than a place or a thing? With a few tools of the trade and some technique, you can have a bar anywhere. Just as they do in a restaurant, bars initiate conviviality. You don't need a lot of space—a bar can be as simple as a silver tray with a few bottles and utensils. Here is what I've learned over many years of drinking:

I. Build a Repertoire: The greatest part about having your own bar is being able to serve only what you love. Like cooking, I say learn the classics and go from there. Basically, drink plenty and drink often, all in the name of research . . .

2. Stay Simple: Instead of flooding your bar with one bottle of everything, edit your collection based on your preferences. Then, learn to prepare your favorite drink or drinks. Much better to do one drink well than many drinks poorly.

3. Let Guests Help Themselves: It can be very nice and comfortable to set up a bar that invites guests to help themselves. They can mix their own drink or mix drinks for other guests. It feels easy and informal.

4. Less Is More: Don't crowd your bar. Remove anything you don't need. Keep it simple and keep it all on a tray to help create a sense of organization.

THE CONTENTS OF MY BAR

UTENSILS	BOTTLES	GARNISHES
I. Jigger (1½ oz to 1 oz)	I. Campari	I. Lemon/Orange Wedges
2. Boston Shaker	2. Aperol	2. Caperberries
3. Julep Strainer	3. Cynar	3. Olives
4. Bar Spoon	4. Pernod	4. Amarena Cherries
5. Muddler	5. Junipero Gin	
6. Bottle Opener	6. Blanton's Bourbon	
7. Corkscrew	7. Ice Glen Vodka from Berkshire Mountain Distillers	
8. Mixing Glass	8. Antica Formula Sweet Vermouth	
9. Ice Bucket	9. Angostura Bitters	
10. Tray		
11. Cocktail Napkins		

Vin Brûlé

Vin brûlé, literally translated, means "burned wine" and is how the French refer to mulled wine. The tradition of warming wine with spices and fruits is ancient, and we keep it alive at Buvette. During the winter we keep a steady stream of vin brûlé in a silver samovar behind the bar and let the smell of winter spices and orange peel perfume the entire restaurant.

[SERVES 4 TO 6]

1 bottle red wine

Zest of 1 orange, removed in large strips

2 large cinnamon sticks, broken into small pieces

2 teaspoons freshly grated nutmeg

½ cup sugar

Combine all of the ingredients in a pot over a medium flame. Bring the mixture to a simmer—be careful not to boil it—and let it cook, stirring occasionally, until the sugar has dissolved and the spices are fragrant. I like to think of it as the moment when the spices begin to sing. Serve warm.

On the Sequencing of Drinking

The custom is to drink white before red, young before old, and light before full wines—unless you are in Japan where they seem to drink everything at once. Either way, I always have enjoyed myself, maybe too much.

Notes on French Wine

VIN NATUREL

There's a lot of attention being paid to "natural wines," an umbrella term that describes any type of wine made without chemicals and with old-school traditions all the way from the planting of the grapes to the bottling of the wine. The wines can be a little bit less predictable than regular wine since so few variables can be controlled. That said, natural wines are exciting precisely because of all of their variation. Like anything that's encouraged to be completely itself, natural wine develops all sorts of wild characteristics. The natural wine movement is full of good stories like that of certified biodynamic winemaker Oliver Cousin, who is a local wine renegade in the Loire Valley. He plows with draft horses, picks grapes by hand, and crushes them by foot. Only ambient yeasts are used and sulfites are never added.

THE TEN FRENCH WINE REGIONS

1. **Alsace** produces aromatic terroir-driven wines grown on the wooded foothills of the Vosges—think choucroute garnie! Grapes include: pinot gris, gewürztraminer, muscat, and Riesling.

2. Wines from the **Jura** are traditional yet highly idiosyncratic, often unfiltered with a uniquely yeasty flavor. Grapes include: chardonnay, ploussard, and trousseau.

3. The **Loire Valley** is known as the garden of France and includes Sancerre, Vouvray, Pouilly-Fumé, Cheverny, and Bourgueil. Wines from the Loire Valley are prized for their fruitiness and fresh clean flavors. Grapes include: sauvignon blanc, muscadet, vouvray, pouilly-fumé, chenin blanc and chenin rouge, and cabernet franc.

4. **Burgundy** is divided into the upper and lower slopes. The more prestigious wines are found on the upper slopes, known as the Côte d'Or, near Dijon. Grapes include: chardonnay for chablis, cabernet sauvignon, and pinot noir. There are some good wines from the lower slopes, near Lyon, including: Aligoté Bouzeron, Pouilly-Fuissé, Meursault, and Pommard. Interestingly, monasteries played a key role in developing the originality of Burgundian wine culture. Monks not only introduced the fundamental concept of terroir, dividing vineyards according to soil, climate, and orientation, but also planted the pinot noir and chardonnay grape varieties as well.

5. Wine has been made in **Beaujolais** for more than 2,000 years, ever since the ancient Greeks founded the city of Marseille in 600 BC. Gamay is the only red grape permitted in Beaujolais and by law all the grapes must be picked by hand.

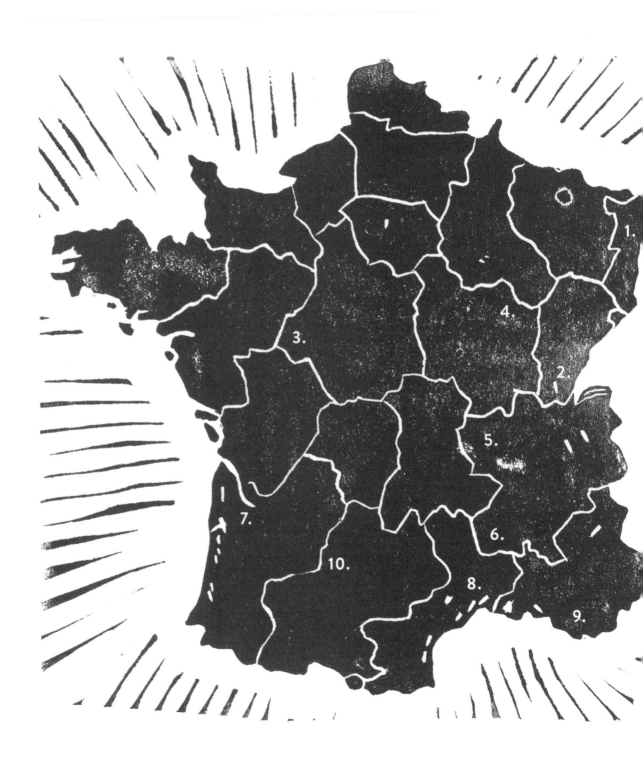

Buvette / The Pleasure of Good Food

6. The **Rhône** valley is known for its warm, rich, and juicy reds. In the north, with its cooler climate and mistral winds, syrah is the only grape grown. In the warmer, dryer climate of the south, they plant grenache, syrah, and mourvèdre.

7. **Bordeaux** is split into two banks—the left is dominated by cabernet, while merlot features prominently on the right.

8. The **Languedoc** borders the Pyrenees and the Mediterranean Sea. It is France's largest and most diverse wine-producing region. Traditional varieties are Carignan, cinsault, mourvèdre, grenache, and malbec.

9. **Provence** is one of the oldest wine-growing regions in the world, established in 600 BC when ancient Greeks first planted syrah grapes outside of Marseille. Look for rosé from this region; it is usually superb.

10. Wine from the **Sud-Ouest** (the southwest) comes from a wide range of growing conditions, from the mild, rainy climate of the Basque Country to the dry, limestone terroirs of Cahors. This area is best known for gastronomic exports like Roquefort, foie gras, and cassoulet. I always try to pair regional food and wine.

HELPFUL THINGS TO KNOW ABOUT WINE

1. Grapes are the only fruit that ferments naturally. When ambient yeast comes into contact with sugar, wine is born.

2. *Vin de pays*, or VDP, is a title given to "country wines." It's been used by savvy vignerons since 1968 as a way to use varietal classification that's free from restrictive AOC laws.

HOW MANY GRAPES IN A GLASS?
720 bottles of wine = 1 ton of grapes
1 bottle of wine = 2.8 pounds of grapes
1 glass of wine = 0.7 pounds of grapes

THE BIGGER THE BOTTLE...
Half bottle or Demi = 0.375 liters
Bouteille normale or Standard = 0.75 liters
Magnum = 1.5 liters
Rehoboam = 4.5 liters
Methuselah = 6 liters
Salmanazar = 9 liters
Balthazar = 12 liters
Nebuchadnezzar = 15 liters

HOW TO REMOVE A RED WINE STAIN

1. First, soak the red wine stain with white wine.

2. Next, cover the stain with baking soda.

3. Let the baking soda dry.

4. Wash the garment as you normally would. Voilà!

ON CORKS

Natural cork wine stoppers are a smart choice. Harvesting the real stuff is an age-old practice that keeps the world's relatively small population of cork oak trees, which can live for hundreds of years, alive. Cork promotes sustainable, economically viable forestry practices around the world. We encourage our guests to throw a cork into the basket of the bicycle that's always parked outside of Buvette for good luck!

ON GLASSES AND WINE TEMPERATURE

To keep your white wines and sparkling wines cool as you drink, hold them by the stem of the glass, but red wines should be held by cupping the glass bowl, which will warm them slightly and help bring out their flavors.

PART 6.

EVENINGS

A FEW EVENING MENUS

A CELEBRATION FOR FRIENDS

Kirs and Chamapgne

❋

Chicken Liver Mousse

Brandade de Morue

Grilled Oysters with Shallots

Pâté de Campagne

Leeks in Vinaigrette

Vichy Carrots

Radicchio with Pine Nuts, Currants, and Aged Balsamic

Slow-Roasted Fennel in Bitter Orange Vinaigrette

Beets with Almonds and Horseradish Crème Fraîche

❋

Roast Chicken

Endive and Radicchio Salad with Pears, Pomegranate, Walnuts, and Roquefort

Cauliflower Gratin

Tartiflette

❋

Flourless Chocolate Cake

Tarte Tatin

Pears Roasted in Red Wine

Roasted Chestnuts and Chocolate-Dipped Gooseberries

VALENTINE'S DAY DINNER FOR A SMALL GROUP OF SINGLE FRIENDS

Negronis

Endive and Radicchio Salad with Pears, Pomegranate, Walnuts, and Roquefort

Risotto Sotto Bosco

Mousse au Chocolat

AN EASY WEEKDAY FAMILY MEAL

Old-Fashioned Lemonade for the Kids and Lemonaris for the Grown-ups

Hachis Parmentier

Grilled Escarole

Spoonfuls of Nutella

How to Time a Meal

A good trick for preparing a meal is to prepare it in reverse. Make dessert first, even a day before. There's no feeling more reassuring than having a bowl of Mousse au Chocolat (page 234) in the fridge, or a Tarte Tatin (page 243) perched on a cake stand ready to go. Then make your main course and side dishes ahead of time, so you don't have to worry about them. For example, a Roast Chicken (page 202) can be cut into pieces and tucked back in the oven to warm up right before serving, and while you've got the oven on, put in the Tartiflette (page 182), until bubbling hot and the cheese is brown and crispy. Planning and cooking like this means that when your guests arrive, you can be putting the final touches on cocktails or snacks, perhaps frying off homemade Rosemary Potato Chips (page 131), knowing that dinner is done and the kitchen is (mostly) clean and all you have to do is relax.

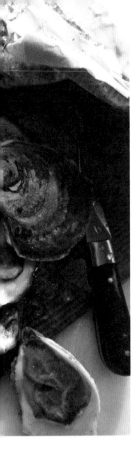

Evenings

There is a communal table at Buvette that seats twelve. In the mornings we use
it as a kitchen table for prep: shelling beans, peeling asparagus, or making
croque-monsieurs. In the evening we seat couples and groups side by side. It isn't
for everyone, but by the looks of it, most guests do enjoy themselves.

For a celebration at the table, we create a feast around one simple roast chicken.
Upon the guests' arrival we greet them with Kirs and a generously stocked table of
charcuterie. There are carved hams and pots of mustard with chilled leeks and
asparagus in vinaigrette. Waiters pass tartinettes with oxtail marmalade
and walnut pesto, not to mention warm schiacciata from the oven. From the kitchen
I often hear bottles of Champagne being opened, sounding like gunfire from the
dining room, a signal the celebration is underway. There are many recipes
here to help you create an informal feast of your own, as well as a few techniques
to make it all the easier.

I remember the first grand meal I made. I was seven years old and I made lunch
for my mother, who was a schoolteacher, and a colleague of hers. Unplanned
and unsolicited, I brought them from the kitchen a tray with two beefsteak tomatoes
filled with a sloppy tuna salad, along with iced teas and cutlery rolled in paper napkins.
My wobbly tomatoes were greeted with smiles—I have come a long way.

Leeks in Vinaigrette

A classic bistro preparation, this is one of my favorite vegetable dishes. Serve these leeks on their own to start a meal, or alongside Roast Chicken (page 202) or crispy Duck Confit (page 140) as an unexpected, beautiful side dish. Note that the longer these sit and marinate in the dressing, the better they get, so feel free to make them ahead.

[SERVES 4]

Coarse salt

1 bunch leeks, white and light green parts only, well washed

½ cup Vinaigrette (page 258)

1 teaspoon Dijon mustard

1 teaspoon whole-grain mustard

Bring a large pot of water to a boil and salt it. Add the leeks and cook until softened, about 15 minutes. To test for doneness, insert a paring knife into one of the leeks—it should be able to go through with barely any resistance.

Transfer the leeks to a plate and let cool to room temperature.

Meanwhile, whisk together the vinaigrette and the mustards.

Cut each leek in half lengthwise, then cut the halves in half crosswise. Place them on a platter, cut side up, and cover with the vinaigrette. Let the leeks sit for at least 10 minutes before serving so that the dressing has a chance to find its way between the leeks' layers.

Buvette / The Pleasure of Good Food

Vichy Carrots

These glazed carrots are said to have originally been made with the famous water from the springs at Vichy in France. While they are usually cooked with just water, butter, and sugar, I like to add sherry vinegar, honey, aromatic shallots, and thyme. If you can find pale yellow carrots and purple ones too, be sure to use those for a striking presentation (see Recipe Note).

[SERVES 4]

1 pound carrots (preferably baby ones, but you can cut regular carrots into lengths roughly ½ inch wide by 2 inches long), peeled and trimmed

Coarse salt

2 tablespoons sherry vinegar

2 tablespoons honey

2 tablespoons extra-virgin olive oil

1 shallot, finely diced

½ teaspoon fresh thyme leaves, finely chopped

Freshly ground black pepper

Put the carrots, a healthy pinch of salt, and a tablespoon of the vinegar into a skillet. Add enough cold water to cover them by half. Set the skillet over high heat and bring the mixture to a boil. Reduce the heat to medium and cook, stirring occasionally, until the carrots are just cooked through, about 15 minutes. If the pan threatens to dry out while they're cooking, simply add an extra splash of water. To test for doneness, insert a paring knife into one of the carrots; it should be able to go through with barely any resistance.

Once the carrots are just cooked through, the water should be nearly evaporated; if it's not, simply pour it off. Add the remaining 1 tablespoon vinegar to the pot along with the honey, olive oil, shallot, and thyme and cook for just a minute or two more to get a nice glaze on the carrots. Season the carrots to taste with salt and pepper. Serve immediately, at room temperature, or refrigerate them and serve cold. They're good all ways!

> RECIPE NOTE
> ### On Cooking Rainbow Carrots
> If you are lucky enough to find rainbow carrots in yellow, purple, red, and orange hues, cook them separately to keep the colors from bleeding.

Radicchio with Pine Nuts, Currants, and Aged Balsamic

Braising tough, bitter radicchio in a simple combination of olive oil and water turns its leaves soft and supple. Serve it with toasted pine nuts, fruity currants, and sweet-and-sour balsamic vinegar as a nod to Sicily, the Italian island that happens to be the largest in the Mediterranean, and where the combination is used frequently in all kinds of dishes.

[SERVES 4]

2 small heads radicchio

¼ cup extra-virgin olive oil

¼ cup water

Coarse salt

2 tablespoons toasted pine nuts

2 tablespoons currants

1 tablespoon good-quality aged balsamic vinegar

Preheat the oven to 450°F.

Quarter each radicchio lengthwise. Be sure to leave the cores intact so that you end up with wedges that are held together at the base.

Place the radicchio wedges in a roasting dish or a skillet, anything that will hold them in an even layer and that can go into the oven. Drizzle with the olive oil and pour in the water. Tightly cover the dish with a lid or aluminum foil and roast in the oven until tender when pierced with a paring knife, about 20 minutes.

Transfer the radicchio to a serving dish and sprinkle with a large pinch of salt. Scatter the pine nuts and currants over the radicchio, and drizzle with the balsamic vinegar.

Serve warm or at room temperature.

On Making Cooking Habitual

To really enjoy cooking, and have it come very easily to you, make it your habit. Once you learn to cook, it becomes intuitive, an extension of your instincts and emotions. But you need good habits to begin with. And trust me, it's much better to learn good ones than break bad ones.

Slow-Roasted Fennel
in Bitter Orange Vinaigrette

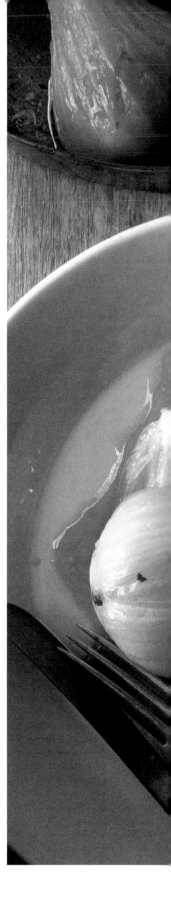

I started making this fennel as a way to use leftover orange juice from breakfast. The orange mixture can be used for all sorts of things, including dressing raw, sliced cabbage, or poaching fish. Serve this fennel as a first course before a large meal, or as a side dish alongside Roast Chicken (page 202) or crispy legs of Duck Confit (page 140).

[SERVES 4]

1 large orange

2 tablespoons sherry vinegar, plus more as needed

2 tablespoons honey, plus more as needed

Pinch coarse salt, plus more as needed

1 small garlic clove, finely minced or puréed on a Microplane grater

1 small dried red chili, or a pinch of red chili flakes

2 fennel bulbs, green stems and fronds removed and reserved for another use

¼ cup extra-virgin olive oil

Preheat the oven to 450°F.

Using a vegetable peeler, remove 3 large strips of zest from the orange and place them into a small saucepan. Set a small sieve over the saucepan. Cut the orange in half and juice it directly into the saucepan through the sieve to catch the seeds and pulp, then discard them. Add the vinegar, honey, salt, garlic, and chili to the orange juice. Stir to combine all of the ingredients and bring to a boil over high heat. Reduce the heat and allow the orange mixture to simmer until just beginning to thicken ever so slightly, 2 to 3 minutes. Remove the pot from the heat, taste for seasoning, and add more salt, honey, or vinegar if you think it needs it. Set the mixture aside.

Cut each fennel bulb in half lengthwise and place the halves, cut side down, in a roasting dish or a skillet, anything that will hold them in an even layer and that can go into the oven. Drizzle with the olive oil and pour over the reserved orange mixture. Tightly cover the dish with a lid or aluminum foil and roast in the oven until the fennel is tender when pierced with a paring knife, about 30 minutes.

Transfer the fennel to a serving dish that has a bit of a lip, and pour over the cooking juices.

Serve warm or at room temperature.

Beets with Almonds and Horseradish Crème Fraîche

In this combination, the almonds enhance the beets' earthiness, and the bracing, creamy horseradish dressing offers not just richness but also a bit of a bite. Be sure not to discard the leafy greens from the beets; they are a wonderful vegetable in and of themselves. Chop beet greens and add to a soup, or slice and sauté them with garlic and chili as you would spinach or any leafy green. Waste not, want not, as they say!

[SERVES 4]

1 bunch beets, leafy greens removed (see note above), but leave 1 or 2 inches of the stems, scrubbed and rinsed

½ cup water

½ cup Vinaigrette (page 258)

3 tablespoons raw almonds, roughly chopped

½ cup crème fraîche

1½ tablespoons prepared horseradish, or 1 tablespoon freshly grated horseradish

2 teaspoons sherry vinegar

Coarse salt

2 tablespoons high-quality, extra-virgin olive oil

Preheat the oven to 425°F.

Place the beets and the water in a baking dish or on a rimmed sheet pan. Roast the beets, turning occasionally, until they're cooked through, about 45 minutes depending on their size. To test for doneness, insert a paring knife into the largest beet—it should be able to go through with barely any resistance.

Let the beets rest until they're cool enough to handle. Trim off and discard the stem ends of the beets and carefully peel the beets. Cut the beets into bite-size wedges and place them into a bowl. Add the vinaigrette and the almonds to the bowl and stir to combine. At this point the beets can be stored for up to a week; they only get better as they marinate in the dressing.

In a small bowl, whisk together the crème fraîche, horseradish, and vinegar and season the mixture with salt.

To serve, dollop the crème fraîche mixture onto the beets and drizzle with the olive oil.

Cooking Vegetables in Parchment Paper: Papillotte and Cartoccio

Cooking and serving vegetables wrapped in parchment paper is a clever way to prepare side dishes. Cooking them this way keeps them off your stovetop and in the oven, so you have more space to do other things. Plus, it steams and roasts them at the same time so they emerge perfectly cooked. Whether or not I've initially cooked vegetables in paper packages, I often serve them that way because I can make the packets far in advance and just pop them into the oven to reheat them when everyone sits at the table. People swoon over the presentation!

To cook vegetables this way, place them on one half of a large piece of parchment paper, drizzle with a little olive oil, and sprinkle with a pinch of salt. Add whatever other seasonings you might like (sliced garlic, herbes de Provence, fresh thyme, etc.), and add a tiny splash of water or wine too. Fold the other half of the parchment paper over the vegetables and crimp the edges to form a packet. (If you're just going to serve cooked vegetables en papillotte, simply wrap them up and don't worry about the olive oil, water, etc.) Place the packets in a 425°F oven and roast the vegetables until they're cooked through to your liking, anywhere from 15 minutes for asparagus to about 1 hour for beets. If you want the paper to really brown, drizzle the outside of it with lemon juice before baking.

Salsify Sweet and Sour

Salsify is sometimes referred to as the oyster plant since, once cooked, its flavor has been likened to oysters. In its raw state, salsify looks like long, brown, dirty carrots. Once peeled, its natural sap emerges, a sign of the sweet final product. You could substitute any firm root vegetable in this dish, including carrots or parsnips, and also feel free to use white wine instead of red. Serve with Roast Chicken (page 202), or grilled quail or rabbit.

[SERVES 4]

4 salsify roots, peeled, trimmed, and cut into 3-inch-long pieces

½ bottle full, rich red wine (a cabernet works nicely)

⅓ cup honey

Two 5-inch sprigs fresh rosemary or thyme

3 large garlic cloves, crushed with the back of your knife or even with your fist (don't even bother peeling them)

½ teaspoon coarse salt

1 cup crumbled blue cheese, such as Roquefort, for serving

Combine all of the ingredients except for the cheese in a saucepan over high heat and bring to a boil. Reduce the heat, and simmer until the salsify is tender when pierced with a paring knife, 20 to 30 minutes. Transfer the salsify to a serving dish.

Bring the cooking liquid in the pot to a boil. Cook until a thick syrup forms, about 5 minutes. Discard the rosemary or thyme and the garlic and pour the reduction over the salsify.

Serve immediately with the blue cheese scattered on top, if you'd like.

Lentils with Kale and Shallots

This hearty lentil dish is all about patience and slow cooking. You want the kale to really cook to the point where it just about loses its physical integrity and all of its freshness is dissolved into the lentils. The effect becomes rich and comforting. And while this is completely vegetarian, I am not. Really, I am just opportunistic and I believe in the freedom of what works well. Which is to say, this would be great with bacon!

[SERVES 4 TO 6]

¼ cup extra-virgin olive oil

3 shallots, peeled and diced

5 garlic cloves, peeled and trimmed

2 dried red chilies or 1 teaspoon red chili flakes

1 bunch kale (preferably lacinato kale, also known as dinosaur kale), finely chopped

1 cup dark lentils (see Recipe Note)

Coarse salt

4 cups water

½ teaspoon freshly grated nutmeg

Crème fraîche, for serving

Some really high-quality, extra-virgin olive oil, for serving

Heat the ¼ cup olive oil in a large pot over medium-high heat. Add the shallots, garlic, chili, and kale and cook, stirring occasionally, until the vegetables are just beginning to soften, about 5 minutes. Add the lentils, a healthy pinch of salt, and the water. Bring the mixture to a boil, reduce the heat, and simmer gently until the lentils and kale are not *just* cooked through, but really soft and lovely, a good hour, maybe even two; it will depend on the age and type of lentil you choose. Splash the mixture with additional water as it cooks if it's threatening to dry out; you want the final product to be moist, but not at all brothy. Just before serving, stir in the nutmeg and season the mixture with salt.

Serve hot or at room temperature with generous spoonfuls of cold crème fraîche and a healthy drizzle of the raw, high-quality, extra-virgin olive oil.

> RECIPE NOTE
> I prefer very dark green, tiny lentils for this dish, often labeled "du Puy" or "Castelluccio." They retain their shape when you cook them and have a wonderfully nutty, earthy flavor. Be sure to pour them out onto a plate before you cook them to look for little stones. While they're rare, you don't want any of your guests or friends breaking a tooth.

Ratatouille

Ratatouille is a traditional vegetable stew from Provence, which is great on its own and also as a filling for sandwiches and omelettes. In fact, one of my favorite sandwiches is a heaping spoonful of ratatouille with sliced, roasted lamb on toast that has been slathered with Aioli (page 264). In the summertime, add a handful of Niçoise olives and roughly torn fresh basil leaves.

[SERVES 4]

¼ cup extra-virgin olive oil

1 small yellow onion, peeled and finely diced

2 plum tomatoes, diced

1 bell pepper (any color!), stemmed, seeded, and cut into ½-inch dice

2 garlic cloves, peeled and minced

Coarse salt

1 large eggplant, peeled and cut into ½-inch dice

1 zucchini, trimmed and cut into ½-inch dice

Pinch red chili flakes

1 teaspoon Herbes de Provence (page 261)

2 teaspoons sherry vinegar

Place the olive oil in a large, heavy pot over medium heat. Add the onion, tomatoes, bell pepper, garlic, and a pinch of salt and cook, stirring occasionally, until the vegetables begin to soften, about 10 minutes. Make sure the heat is high enough to keep everything cooking, but not so high that the vegetables color; you want them to sweat, not brown. Add the eggplant along with another pinch of salt and cook until the eggplant begins to soften, another 10 minutes. Lastly, add the zucchini, along with the chili flakes and herbes de Provence. If the mixture is looking a little dry, add another tablespoon of olive oil. Stir and cook for a final 15 minutes, or until all of the vegetables are wonderfully soft and yielding. Stir in the vinegar and season with more salt, if needed.

Serve warm, at room temperature, or even cold. Ratatouille only gets better the longer it sits, and it keeps for up to a week in a sealed container in the refrigerator.

Grilled Escarole

This is spectacularly easy, quite mouthwatering, and
works as both a first course before an entrée or as a side
dish. Escarole is part of the chicory family and has a
pleasant bitterness to it. Note that while the outer leaves
of the escarole are not used in this preparation, they
should not be discarded. Some particularly good uses
include Poached Eggs over Scafata (page 13) or Soupe
au Pistou (page 104).

[SERVES 4]

1 head escarole, outer leaves removed
and saved, thoroughly washed

Extra-virgin olive oil

Coarse salt

½ cup pitted, crushed green olives

Get your grill going. If you're using charcoal, you're looking for
a not-too-hot fire (I like to think of the coals as being "soft," which
is to say they should be halfway through burning). If you're using a
gas grill, set the heat to medium. If you're using a grill pan indoors,
set it over medium-low heat.

Shake the escarole dry. Cut it lengthwise straight through the
core into 4 wedges. Drizzle each wedge with plenty of olive oil,
about 1½ tablespoons per wedge, and season aggressively with salt.
Grill the wedges, turning only once, until wilted and charred in
spots, about 10 minutes altogether.

Transfer the escarole to a serving platter, give it a healthy drizzle
of olive oil, and scatter the olives over the top. Serve immediately.

Cauliflower Gratin

This gratin works with all sorts of vegetables, including endive, romanesco, broccoli, Swiss chard, or even just chard stems. It makes a nice and simple lunch when served with a green salad, or it works as a decadent side dish too. The gratin can also be assembled ahead of time, stored in the refrigerator, and popped into the oven just before sitting down to dinner, making it great for entertaining.

[SERVES 6]

Coarse salt

1 large head cauliflower

6 tablespoons (¾ stick) unsalted butter

¼ cup plus 1 tablespoon unbleached all-purpose flour

2 teaspoons freshly grated nutmeg, plus more as needed

4¼ cups whole milk

4 large fresh sage leaves, thinly sliced

Freshly ground black pepper

1½ cups grated Gruyère cheese

Preheat the oven to 375°F.

Bring a large pot of water to a boil and season aggressively with salt. Meanwhile, remove the green outer leaves from the cauliflower and roughly chop them. Cut the cauliflower into florets. Add the cauliflower and the greens to the boiling water and cook just until tender, about 3 minutes. Drain the cauliflower and the greens, place them in a bowl, and set them aside.

Meanwhile, combine the butter, flour, nutmeg, and 2 teaspoons of salt in a heavy saucepan over medium heat. Cook, stirring, until barely browned, 3 to 4 minutes. Gradually stir in the milk and cook, stirring constantly, until the mixture thickens, 3 to 4 minutes. Remove the béchamel sauce from the heat.

Pour the sauce over the reserved cauliflower, add the sage, and stir to combine. Season to taste with salt, pepper, and additional nutmeg if you think it needs it; the seasoning will depend on the size of the cauliflower.

Transfer the cauliflower to a large, 10-inch gratin dish or skillet, or to six individual gratin dishes. Top the dish (or dishes) evenly with the grated cheese and bake until bubbling hot and golden brown, about 20 minutes.

Tartiflette

Rich and comforting, *tartiflette*, a sort of rustic gratin of potatoes, onions, bacon, and plenty of dairy (crème fraîche, a generous layer of Reblochon cheese, and a final pour of cream), is not for anyone with a small appetite or an inclination toward moderation. You can prepare the potato mixture up to a few days in advance and then simply dress it with the dairy and send it into the oven just before you sit down to dinner.

[SERVES 4 HEARTILY]

¼ pound sliced bacon, cut crosswise into ½-inch lardons

1 yellow onion, peeled and diced

8 leaves fresh sage, roughly chopped

1½ pounds small, waxy yellow potatoes, peeled and cut into bite-size pieces

½ teaspoon freshly grated nutmeg

½ cup crème fraîche

Coarse salt

⅓ pound Reblochon cheese (or any soft, washed-rind cheese such as Brie)

2 tablespoons heavy cream

Preheat the oven to 425°F.

Place the bacon into a large, heavy, ovenproof skillet over medium heat. Cook, stirring occasionally, until all of the fat has nearly rendered and the bacon is just beginning to crisp, 5 to 10 minutes.

Add the onion to the skillet and cook, stirring occasionally, until softened, another 10 minutes.

Add the sage and potatoes and cook, stirring occasionally, until the onions are quite brown and sticky, almost like a jam, and the potatoes are just cooked through, 20 to 25 minutes. Stir the nutmeg and crème fraîche into the potato mixture and season with salt.

At this point you can transfer the potato mixture to a gratin dish or individual ramekins or simply leave them in the skillet.

Blanket the potato mixture with slices of the cheese and evenly pour over the cream. Place the skillet in the oven and bake until the cheese has melted and browned, about 15 minutes.

A NOTE ON WINE

A wine from the very alpine Savoy region of France works really well with this hearty dish—I especially like to serve it with either a red wine made from mondeuse grapes, which have a real barnyard quality, or a white wine made with jacquère grapes.

Potato Pancakes

My mother was not a great cook, but she could make delicious potato pancakes—and with a box grater no less. This was one of my favorite meals as a child, especially when topped with homemade Roasted Applesauce (page 244). Other serving ideas are Brandade de Morue (page 217) or crème fraîche and slices of smoked salmon. They're also really nice alongside Roasted Heirloom Apples Filled with Pork Sausage (page 201).

[MAKES 1½ DOZEN POTATO PANCAKES]

2 russet potatoes, peeled

½ yellow onion, peeled and very finely chopped

2 egg yolks, beaten

1 teaspoon coarse salt, plus extra for sprinkling on the cooked potato pancakes

½ teaspoon freshly ground black pepper

½ cup cornstarch

Oil, for frying (corn, peanut, canola, or grapeseed oil all work well)

Coarsely grate the potatoes into a colander. Squeeze the potatoes so that they release most of their starchy liquid, but no need to go overboard here—a little liquid is okay. Transfer the potatoes to a large mixing bowl and stir in the onion, egg yolks, salt, pepper, and cornstarch and combine thoroughly.

Heat ¼ inch of oil in a large, heavy skillet over medium-high heat. Once the oil is hot, place heaping tablespoonfuls of the potato mixture into the oil, leaving plenty of space between the pancakes. Using the back of your spoon, gently flatten each heap of potato so that the pancakes are 2 to 3 inches in diameter. Cook until the undersides are browned, about 3 minutes. Carefully turn each pancake and cook until brown on the opposite side, another few minutes. Transfer the cooked pancakes to a paper towel–lined plate and season with a pinch of salt.

Continue cooking the pancakes, in batches, until you've used up all of the potato mixture, adding more oil to the skillet as needed.

Serve hot. These can be kept warm in a low oven, or reheated in a hot oven, so feel free to make them in advance.

Aligot

Combining roughly equal parts potatoes and cheese, this smooth, elastic mixture is like potato fondue. *Aligot* is traditionally made with Cantal cheese, but any soft, young, cow's-milk cheese will work. At Buvette, since our tables are so small and we don't have space for big plates, we serve our aligot on garlic-rubbed toast and drape it with thin slices of prosciutto. Aligot also goes well with country ham, grilled sausages, or a Roast Chicken (page 202). Note that any leftover aligot—unlikely—can be heated up in a pan with an extra splash of cream.

[SERVES 4 HEARTILY]

1¼ pounds Yukon gold potatoes, scrubbed

½ cup heavy cream

2 garlic cloves, peeled

Coarse salt

Freshly ground black pepper

3 cups grated Cantal or Jack cheese

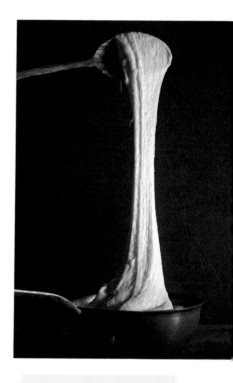

Place the potatoes in a large pot of salted, cool water, and bring to a boil over high heat. Cook until they're tender, about 30 minutes. Drain the potatoes and set them aside to cool slightly.

Meanwhile, pour the cream into a small saucepan and, using a Microplane grater, grate the garlic into the cream. Heat the cream over medium heat until it's quite hot, but not boiling. Keep the cream warm while you continue with the potatoes.

While the potatoes are still warm, peel them (see Recipe Notes page 197) and pass them through a food mill or a *tamis* (see Recipe Notes page 197) into a clean pot or large skillet. Pour the hot cream into the potatoes and stir to combine. Season the potatoes to taste with salt and pepper, then set the pot over low heat. While stirring constantly and quite aggressively, add the cheese to the potatoes a handful at a time. The mixture will get thick and almost glutinous. Between the stirring and the gentle heat, the cheese will begin to really melt into the potatoes and the two will become a single, uniform, remarkably elastic mixture. It will take 3 to 5 minutes, once all the cheese has been added, to achieve this texture.

Serve immediately.

Stop and Listen Moments
When I opened up Buvette I put a sign in the window that said "Aligot," hoping to attract customers who knew the dish and loved it as much as I do. A woman came in and said that aligot comes from her hometown, and she walked back into the kitchen and gave me a lesson on how to make it her way. If you love cooking classic dishes, as I do, but didn't grow up in the places your most beloved dishes come from, fear not. Just get yourself as close to the source as possible . . . and listen and watch.

Pommes Vigneron

Pommes vigneron translates to "winemaker's potatoes" and while it's a decadent side dish, it can also stand on its own as the main attraction. Traditionally it's been considered an all-in-one meal: a combination of hearty potatoes with some meat that can be cut into large wedges and tucked into a lunch pail, ready for a day of picking grapes. To round out to a complete meal, serve this with a salad of shredded cabbage dressed with mustard, vinegar, and oil.

[SERVES 4]

3 tablespoons unsalted butter, melted

1 large shallot, peeled and finely diced

2 garlic cloves, peeled and finely minced

2 teaspoons fresh thyme leaves, finely chopped

1 teaspoon coarse salt

½ teaspoon freshly ground black pepper

1 pound Yukon gold potatoes (about 4 medium potatoes), peeled

4 slices bacon

1 cup coarsely grated Comté cheese (about 4 ounces), or substitute a mild Gruyère or Jarlsberg cheese

Preheat the oven to 400°F.

In a large mixing bowl, stir together the melted butter, shallot, garlic, thyme, salt, and pepper. Set the mixture aside.

Using a mandoline or a sharp knife, thinly slice the potatoes into disks that are about ⅛ inch thick (which is to say thin, but not paper thin). Add the potatoes to the bowl with the butter mixture and stir to combine, making sure the aromatic mixture is evenly dispersed among the potato slices.

Lay the strips of bacon across a small, 6- to 8-inch diameter skillet or similar size baking dish so that they overlap in the center and spiral outward. The majority of the bacon will cover the bottom of the skillet and the ends should hang over the edge.

Place a quarter of the potato mixture over the bacon and sprinkle with one-third of the cheese. Repeat this layering until you've used up all of the potatoes and the cheese. Cover the exposed potatoes with the exposed ends of the bacon strips. Cut a piece of parchment paper into a circle just slightly larger than the skillet, press the paper on top of the bacon, and transfer the skillet to the oven.

Bake until the potatoes are cooked through, the exposed bacon is nice and crisp, and the entire surface is browned, about 1 hour.

Cut into wedges and serve hot or at room temperature.

Risotto with Meyer Lemon

The action of making risotto is what I think of as "real cooking" since it requires your attention the whole time you're making it. More than any other dish I can think of, when risotto hits the table, it's an expression of the cook's skill. Luckily, making risotto, while it does entail patience, isn't all that difficult. This simple lemon variation is especially elegant.

[SERVES 4]

4 tablespoons extra-virgin olive oil

1 shallot, peeled and finely chopped

1 cup high-quality risotto rice

¼ cup dry white wine

Coarse salt

3 to 4 cups boiling water

2 lemons (preferably Meyer lemons)

1 sprig fresh basil

1 cup coarsely grated Parmigiano-Reggiano cheese, plus more for serving

Warm 1 tablespoon of the olive oil in a large saucepan over medium-high heat. Add the shallot and cook, stirring, until the shallot just begins to soften, about 2 minutes. Add the rice and cook, stirring a bit, until it turns opaque and starts to make a faint popping sound, just a minute or two. Add the white wine and a pinch of salt and cook until the wine has nearly evaporated, about 2 minutes. Add a cup of the boiling water and cook, stirring continuously, until the water has nearly evaporated. You will know when to add more water when the surface of the rice is coated with small bubbles—it's not unlike knowing when to flip a pancake. Repeat the process with a second cup of the boiling water and the zest and juice of one of the lemons. Once that second cup of water has nearly cooked off, add a third cup of water and the basil sprig and cook until the liquid is nearly evaporated.

Test the rice by tasting it—it should be just cooked through, but still have a bit of a bite. If it's too uncooked, add ¼ cup of water. Depending on the cooking temperature and the type and age of the rice, it may or may not need it. Trust your instincts.

When the rice is just cooked through, about 20 minutes of cooking altogether, turn off the heat, remove and discard the basil, and vigorously mix in the remaining 3 tablespoons olive oil along with the cheese and the zest and juice from the second lemon. This final vigorous mix will help encourage all of the rice's starch to get to its fullest, most creamy and decadent potential. The cheese doesn't hurt! Season the risotto to taste with more salt, if needed.

Serve immediately with a little extra Parmigiano-Reggiano.

RECIPE NOTE

On Meyer Lemons

As a kid in California, my friends and I would reach through the schoolyard fence to steal Meyer lemons, which we used as lemon bombs. I can't believe we used to have lemon wars! I have now learned to appreciate these special lemons as an incredible ingredient with the most floral, fragrant flavor. If you can find them at your greengrocer, it's worth trying them.

Natural Hand Sanitizer

Take it from someone who has spent hours upon hours cleaning artichokes: don't let juiced lemons go to waste. Lemons are a remarkable cleaning device. The juice and oils are very good for your cuticles and take the strong smells of food away. Use them to refresh your hands by rubbing them across your nails and palms, especially after cleaning artichokes, garlic, or fish. They work so well that you won't want to wait to have juiced lemons around.

Risotto with Green Apples, Sage, and Fontina

Hunting down recipes, whether in old books or in-person conversations, is a fine way to collect stories. I found this old-fashioned risotto in the 1962 edition of *Le Ricette Regionali Italiane* by Anna Gosetti della Salda. The ever-so-sweet combination of apples and sage makes this an unexpected and welcome option for brunch. If you serve it for dinner, feel free to make it a bit more savory by cooking it in bacon fat and throwing in a piece of smoked prosciutto for extra flavor.

[SERVES 4]

2 apples (preferably Golden Delicious or Granny Smith), stemmed, cored, and cut into matchsticks

½ cup white wine, preferably Riesling

5 tablespoons unsalted butter

¼ cup chopped shallots

10 fresh sage leaves, roughly chopped

1 cup high-quality risotto rice

Coarse salt

3 to 4 cups boiling water

⅔ cup diced Fontina cheese

½ cup coarsely grated Parmigiano-Reggiano cheese, plus extra for serving

Put the apples and the wine in a small bowl and set aside while you begin the risotto.

Melt 3 tablespoons of the butter in a large saucepan over medium-high heat. Add the shallots and the sage and cook, stirring occasionally, until just beginning to soften, 2 to 3 minutes. Add the rice and cook, stirring a bit, until it turns opaque and starts to make a faint popping sound, just a minute or two. Add the white wine that the apples have been soaking in, and reserve the apples. Cook until the wine has nearly all evaporated, about 2 minutes. Add a pinch of salt and a cup of the boiling water and cook, stirring continuously, until the water has nearly evaporated. Repeat the process with a second cup of the boiling water, and when that has nearly evaporated, add a third cup of water and the reserved apples. You will know when to add more water when the surface of the rice is coated with small bubbles—it's not unlike knowing when to flip a pancake. Cook, stirring, until this last addition of water has nearly evaporated.

Test the rice by tasting it—it should be just cooked through, but still have a bit of a bite. If it's too undercooked, add ¼ cup of water. Depending on the cooking temperature and the type and age of the rice, it may or may not need it. Trust your instincts. »CONTINUES

When the rice is just cooked through, about 20 minutes of cooking altogether, turn off the heat and vigorously mix in the remaining 2 tablespoons butter along with both of the cheeses. This final vigorous mix will help encourage all of the rice's starch to get to its fullest, most creamy and decadent potential. The cheese doesn't hurt! Season the risotto to taste with more salt, if needed, and serve immediately with a little extra Parmigiano-Reggiano.

Risotto Sotto Bosco

This unique risotto is meant to look like *sotto bosco*, or "the forest's floor." The ultimate forager's risotto, this is made with everything you would find on a walk through the woods in autumn, including fresh porcini mushrooms, a mixture of wild herbs, and a handful of berries. Brought together in a single pot, the eccentric combination of ingredients calls to mind the old adage "What grows together, goes together."

[SERVES 4]

4 tablespoons (½ stick) unsalted butter

1 small shallot, peeled and minced

2 firm, fresh porcini mushrooms, cleaned and sliced (about 1½ ounces)

4 fresh sage leaves, chopped

1 teaspoon fresh thyme leaves, minced

Leaves from 1 small sprig fresh rosemary, minced

1 cup high-quality risotto rice

½ cup dry white wine

Coarse salt

3 to 4 cups boiling water

½ cup grated Parmigiano-Reggiano cheese, plus more for serving

Small handful fresh blueberries and/or blackberries

Melt 2 tablespoons of the butter in a heavy pot over medium-high heat. Add the shallot, porcinis, and herbs and cook, stirring occasionally, until just softened and beginning to turn golden brown, about 4 minutes. Add the rice and cook until it turns opaque and starts to make a faint popping sound, just a minute or two. Add the white wine to the pot and cook until almost all of the liquid has evaporated. Add a pinch of salt and 1 cup of the boiling water and cook, stirring continuously, until the water has nearly evaporated. Repeat the process with a second cup of the boiling water, and when that has nearly evaporated, add a third cup. You will know when to add more water when the surface of the rice is coated with small bubbles—it's not unlike knowing when to flip a pancake. Cook, stirring, until this last addition of water has nearly evaporated.

Test the rice by tasting it—it should be just cooked through, but still have a bit of a bite. If it's too undercooked, add ¼ cup of water. Depending on the cooking temperature and the type and age of the rice, it may or may not need it. Trust your instincts.

When the rice is just cooked through, about 20 minutes of cooking altogether, turn off the heat and vigorously mix in the remaining 2 tablespoons butter along with the cheese. Fold in the berries, and season the risotto to taste with salt.

Serve immediately, with an extra dusting of Parmigiano-Reggiano on each portion.

On Tending to Your Pots
In order to be a good cook, it helps to be observant, patient, and in charge. To tend to the pots and ovens, don't be afraid to lean over, to stir whatever's in there, to spread it out and see what's happening. Most beginning cooks tend to be intimidated by everything happening on the stove—it helps to remember you are in charge of the food and not the other way around.

Steak Tartare

This recipe depends entirely on the quality of your meat. Think of it like beef sashimi—only the highest quality will do. Although high quality means high price, this is a great way to stretch an expensive steak since one pound will provide enough tartare for four people. While most steak tartare recipes include a raw egg yolk, I purposely omit it from mine. I find the raw egg muddles the flavor of the raw beef.

[SERVES 4]

1 teaspoon Dijon mustard

1 teaspoon Worcestershire sauce

3 dashes Tabasco sauce

5 tablespoons extra-virgin olive oil

2 tablespoons capers, drained and very finely chopped

4 cornichons, very finely chopped

1 shallot, peeled and very finely chopped (about 2 tablespoons)

2 garlic cloves, peeled and puréed using a Microplane grater (or mashed to a paste)

Coarse salt

Freshly ground black pepper

One 1-pound New York strip steak (2 inches thick), all excess fat trimmed off and discarded

For serving: grilled toast, drizzled with extra-virgin olive oil; a handful of extra cornichons; olives; a fistful of wild arugula or a few leaves of butter lettuce; a hard-boiled egg or an *oeuf mollet*; a couple of anchovies; and some radishes

In a mixing bowl, whisk together the Dijon, Worcestershire sauce, Tabasco, and olive oil. Stir in the capers, cornichons, shallot, and garlic. Season the dressing to taste with salt and pepper and set aside.

Fill a large bowl with ice and a bit of water. Place a slightly smaller metal mixing bowl on top of the ice bath, and place the whole setup next to your cutting board. Using a sharp knife, cut the meat against the grain into thin, but not too thin, slices (about ¼ inch thick). Place 4 or so slices of steak on top of each other in a little pile and cut the slices into long strands, then cut the strands crosswise into a rough dice. Place the meat into the bowl that's sitting on the ice water as you cut, continuing until you've diced all of the meat.

When you're ready to serve, pour the dressing over the meat and season with an additional pinch of salt and a few grinds of black pepper. Stir gently to combine and serve immediately alongside grilled toast that's been drizzled with olive oil and with a handful of extra cornichons on the plate too. Olives are nice as well, and if you want to make a real meal out of the tartare, add a fistful of wild arugula to the plate

or a few leaves of beautiful butter lettuce and some radishes. A hard-boiled egg or an *oeuf mollet* (a soft-boiled egg that's got a set, but still soft yolk) and a couple of anchovies would be welcome on the plate as well.

RECIPE NOTE

The dressing is not unlike a salsa verde and can stand on its own. It's also great with fish, grilled chicken, etc.

Meatballs

Many years ago, a talented actor from *The Sopranos* gave me his grandmother's beloved meatball recipe. He went into great detail about her method and encouraged me to try the meatballs. Indeed, they sounded delicious, and quickly became a signature dish in many of my kitchens.

[SERVES 4 GENEROUSLY]

Tomato Sauce (page 269)

¼ cup dried currants

2 tablespoons sherry vinegar

2 tablespoons extra-virgin olive oil

1 yellow onion, peeled and finely diced

3 garlic cloves, crushed

2 tablespoons fresh basil leaves, finely chopped

1 tablespoon finely chopped fresh flat-leaf parsley

3 cups homemade fresh bread crumbs (page 268)

½ cup whole milk

½ pound ground pork

½ pound ground veal

¼ pound ground beef

¼ pound ground mortadella

¼ cup pine nuts, toasted

Pinch red chili flakes

1 teaspoon dried oregano

½ teaspoon freshly grated nutmeg

1½ teaspoons coarse salt

½ teaspoon freshly ground black pepper

½ cup finely grated Parmigiano-Reggiano cheese

2 large eggs, beaten

Flour, for dredging

Oil, for frying (corn, peanut, vegetable, canola, or grapeseed oil all work well)

In a large pot, bring the tomato sauce to a simmer and keep it warm over low heat.

Meanwhile, put the currants and sherry vinegar in a small bowl and cover them with warm water. Let the currants soak for 10 minutes, drain, and set aside.

Warm the olive oil in a large sauté pan over medium heat. Add the onion, garlic, basil, and parsley and cook, stirring occasionally, until softened, about 10 minutes. Remove the aromatics from the heat and set aside to cool.

Meanwhile, put the bread crumbs in a large bowl with the milk and stir to combine so that the mixture is nice and soft. Add all of the ground meats and the cooled aromatic mixture, along with the drained currants, pine nuts, chili flakes, oregano, nutmeg, salt, pepper, cheese, and eggs.

Generously coat the surface of a baking sheet with flour. To form the meatballs,

grab a handful of the meat and squeeze it to allow for some of the meat to escape from the top of your hand just beside your thumb. This squeezing will create wonderfully rustic, not-too-perfectly-round meatballs that you can allow to simply fall to the baking sheet as you make them. This method will naturally portion the meatballs and keep you from overhandling them, which is what causes most tough meatballs.

Give the baking sheet a shake, allowing the meatballs to roll around and coat themselves in the flour. A meatball that is not necessarily smooth, round, and uniform will have a delicious crunchy surface with dimples, which will hold more sauce.

Set a large sauté pan over medium heat and coat it with a shallow layer of vegetable oil. Add enough meatballs to fit in a single, uncrowded layer and fry until browned on all sides, about 5 minutes. Transfer the meatballs to a paper towel–lined plate to drain and continue frying off the meatballs, in batches, until you've browned them all.

Carefully transfer the meatballs to the simmering tomato sauce and finish cooking them in the sauce for 20 minutes.

RECIPE NOTES

1. These meatballs freeze beautifully in their sauce, so feel free to double the recipe and stow some away for a rainy day.

2. Remember that miniature meatballs are great for cocktail parties.

Hachis Parmentier

This humble, old, quaint dish is a French shepherd's pie of spiced, ground meat topped with mashed potatoes. I like to imagine it being served in cafeterias to schoolchildren. You can make the *hachis* in one large baking dish, or divide it among individual gratin dishes or ramekins, so everyone gets one for him- or herself. With a simple salad and a basket of bread, dinner is served.

[SERVES 4]

10 allspice berries

1½ teaspoons whole black peppercorns

1 tablespoon fennel seeds

1 tablespoon coriander seeds

2 tablespoons extra-virgin olive oil

1 pound ground beef (at least 20 percent fat)

1 small carrot, peeled and finely diced

1 small celery stalk, finely diced

1 small red onion, peeled and finely diced

Coarse salt

½ cup white wine

2 cups water

2 pounds Yukon gold potatoes

½ cup heavy cream

4 tablespoons (½ stick) unsalted butter

Combine the allspice berries, peppercorns, fennel seeds, and coriander seeds in a coffee grinder or spice mill and process them to a fine powder. Set the spice mixture aside.

Heat the olive oil in a large sauté pan over medium-high heat. Crumble in the meat and cook, stirring occasionally, until it renders off most of its fat and starts to take on a lovely brown color, 10 to 15 minutes. Add the reserved spice mixture and the carrot, celery, and onion to the meat and cook, stirring occasionally, until the vegetables are softened and the mixture is incredibly fragrant, about 10 minutes.

Add a teaspoon of salt to the meat mixture along with the white wine. Increase the heat to high and let the mixture boil until the wine has nearly evaporated, about 5 minutes. Add the water to the pan and let the mixture come to a boil. Reduce the heat and allow the mixture to simmer, skimming off and discarding any fat that rises to the surface. Cook until the mixture becomes concentrated and the liquid has nearly evaporated, about 30 minutes. Season the meat to taste with salt and set it aside.

While the meat mixture is cooking, prepare the potato purée. Put the potatoes into a large saucepan filled with cold water and bring to a boil over high heat. Let the potatoes cook until they're completely soft, about 25 minutes. Test them by piercing them with a paring knife, but don't overdo it; you don't want the potatoes to get waterlogged. When the potatoes are cooked through, drain them in a colander.

Peel the potatoes (see Recipe Notes) and press them through a tamis (see Recipe Notes) or pass them through a potato ricer or a food mill into a large bowl.

Preheat the oven to 400°F.

Meanwhile, warm the cream and the butter in a small saucepan until the butter has melted, then vigorously mix them into the potatoes. Season the potatoes to taste with salt and set them aside.

To assemble the final dish, spread the meat out in a thin, even layer either in a large baking dish or among four individual gratin dishes. Spread the potato purée evenly over the meat. Bake in the oven until the potatoes are browned on top, about 20 minutes. Serve immediately.

RECIPE NOTES

On Peeling Hot Potatoes

While there's something comical about handling a hot potato, there's nothing efficient about trying to peel one. To overcome this without wasting the time it takes for a potato to cool, I simply stab a potato with a fork and hold the handle of the fork, spinning it so I can use a small paring knife in my other hand to quickly and easily peel the potato without having to actually hold it. How cool!

What's a Tamis?

A wonderful kitchen utensil often used in restaurant kitchens, but rarely in home kitchens, a tamis looks a bit like a cake pan but with a fine-mesh sieve for a base. Soft foods, like cooked potatoes, get pushed through, using a wooden spoon or a plastic scraper to help the process. The result is an incredibly smooth, silky purée that doesn't require an appliance, engine, or button.

Choucroute Garnie

Don't be fooled by the elaborate name of this incredibly simple dish—
it means "garnished sauerkraut" and is just cabbage adorned with a bit
of pork. In my version, I warm a bed of good sauerkraut with hard cider
and a few crushed juniper berries and then tuck in bits of leftover pork.
Below I include a step for roasting pork belly since it's incredibly tasty
and easy to prepare, but it's in no way required. Use whatever you like
and whatever you might have on hand.

[SERVES 4]

1 teaspoon coarse salt

1 teaspoon whole black peppercorns

1 teaspoon fennel seeds

2 pounds pork belly, skin intact if possible

4 cups sauerkraut (see sidebar, opposite), rinsed and drained

1 cup high-quality hard apple cider or beer, plus more as needed

5 juniper berries, crushed

1 tablespoon sugar (optional, depending on sweetness of cider)

1 pound leftover cooked pork (ham, shank, shoulder, sausages, etc.), thickly sliced

Mustard, for serving

Preheat the oven to 325°F. Line a baking sheet with aluminum foil.

Coarsely grind the salt, peppercorns, and fennel together in a coffee grinder and
rub the mixture all over the pork belly. Place the pork belly on the prepared baking
sheet and roast in the oven until the fat has rendered significantly, the skin is
browned and crisp, and the meat is tender, 2 to 3 hours depending on the thickness
of the belly. Cut the meat into thick slices and set it aside.

Meanwhile, combine the sauerkraut, cider, and juniper berries in a large pot and
bring it to a boil over high heat, then reduce the heat so that it's just barely at a simmer. Taste the sauerkraut and add the sugar if you think it needs it, and salt too; it
all depends on the flavor of the sauerkraut and sweetness of the cider you're using.

Tuck the reserved pork belly into the sauerkraut along with the additional cooked
pork and simmer everything together until the meat is warmed through and the
sauerkraut is soft, at least 20 minutes, but possibly up to 2 hours. The longer it goes,
the more succulent it gets, and feel free to add a splash more cider as it cooks if needed.

Serve warm, with plenty of mustard.

A NOTE ON WINE

Drink Alsatian wine such as gewürztraminer or Riesling with choucroute garnie,
which also comes from Alsace. It's nice to pair the dish with its neighborhood wine.

RECIPE NOTE

The Best Ever Leftover Sandwich

If choucroute garnie is the best possible way to use up leftover bits of pork, then a choucroute garnie sandwich is the best use of leftover leftovers. For this, one of the most satisfying, incredibly wonderful sandwiches ever, spread both cut sides of a crusty ciabatta roll with Dijon mustard and stuff it full of warm, leftover sauerkraut and whatever bits of pork belly, pork shank, ham, anything!, that are left too. This sandwich is reason alone to make choucroute garnie.

On Sauerkraut: How to Buy It and How to Make It

This dish is all about the cabbage—the meat is just the garnish. Therefore, it's essential that you use sauerkraut with good crunch and tremendous flavor. For local, artisanal sauerkraut, check out what's available at your farmers' market. Sometimes I do a quick sauerkraut à la minute. For that, simply slice half a green cabbage, put it in a large bowl, and pour boiling water over it. Let it sit in the hot water for a minute, then drain it. In a separate bowl, whisk together 3 tablespoons of white vinegar with 3 tablespoons of water, 2 tablespoons of sugar, 1 teaspoon of salt, and a few crushed juniper berries. Pour this mixture over the barely wilted cabbage and stir to combine. Let it sit for at least 1 hour before eating. This makes a very nice, fresh sauerkraut that's especially lovely on sandwiches. You can cook it down for choucroute garnie, but really it's best as a crunchy salad.

Roasted Heirloom Apples
Filled with Pork Sausage

A simple but special dish, these stuffed apples, scented with sage, are best served in the fall when small Lady apples are available at the farmers' market. These go very well with roasted potatoes, Lentils with Kale and Shallots (page 176), Pommes Vigneron (page 186), or any other hearty side dish.

[SERVES 4]

A dozen Lady apples or 4 Gala apples

Coarse salt

Freshly ground black pepper

1 pound cotechino or other fresh, fatty, spicy Italian sausage, removed from its casing (check out dartagnan.com)

2 tablespoons unsalted butter, cut into small pieces

8 to 10 fresh sage leaves, torn in half if large

½ to ¾ bottle white wine

Preheat the oven to 400°F.

If you're using Lady apples, scoop the core and seeds and a little bit of apple flesh out of each one using a teaspoon, making cups out of the apples, each with a substantial space for plenty of filling. If you're using regular apples, cut them in half crosswise and then scoop the core from the center of each and remove the stems, forming 8 cups.

Season the prepared apples with salt and pepper and evenly divide the sausage meat among them, filling each one with enough sausage to make a small mound of meat. Season the sausage with additional salt and pepper and nestle the stuffed apples in an ovenproof skillet or roasting dish that holds them snugly in an even layer.

Scatter the butter over and in between the apples, and tuck the sage leaves among them. Pour enough wine into the skillet (or dish) to almost cover the apples. Roast in the oven until the apples can easily be pierced with a knife, about 1 hour.

Poulet Rôti

This is a simple roast chicken, and that is why it is good. It is almost even better served as a salad with haricots verts and potatoes in mustard vinaigrette (page 258).

[SERVES 4]

1 tablespoon fennel seeds

1 tablespoon Herbes de Provence (page 261)

1 tablespoon coarse salt

One 3- to 4-pound chicken, patted
dry with paper towels

Using a mortar and pestle, or in a coffee grinder, coarsely grind the fennel seeds, herbes de Provence, and salt. Evenly season the chicken with the mixture, inside and out, really massaging it into all of the crevices. Let the chicken sit for at least an hour at room temperature, or in a sealed plastic bag in the refrigerator for up to 3 days.

When you are ready to cook the chicken, preheat the oven to 425°F, place the chicken in a skillet or a roasting dish—anything, really—and set it in the oven. Roast until the thigh registers 165°F on a meat thermometer, about 1 hour and 15 minutes. Let it rest for at least 10 minutes before carving and eating it. No need to truss, baste, anything. Just season and cook. End of story.

On Seasoning White Meats
Dried fennel pollen is one of my favorite herbs, but it's hard to find in America and very expensive. Grinding fennel seeds with a bit of salt mimics it, and the mixture is terrific, not just on chicken, but on any white meat, including pork, fish, rabbit, and veal.

Cassoulet

A rich mixture of meats, vegetables, and beans simmered together for hours, cassoulet is perhaps the best consolation in cold weather. This hearty, one-pot dish is perfect for a party, especially since not only can you make it the day before, but it's also better if you do. Note that the beans have to be soaked overnight before cooking, so be sure to plan ahead.

[SERVES 6 TO 8]

3 tablespoons extra-virgin olive oil or duck fat

1 pound pork spareribs, cut into small sections (2 ribs to a section)

1 pound garlic pork sausage, cut into 3-inch pieces (check out salumeriabiellese.com)

½ pound unsmoked bacon or pork belly, cut into thick lardons

Coarse salt

Freshly ground black pepper

1 leek, white and light green parts only, well washed and diced

1 celery stalk, diced

1 yellow onion, peeled and diced

5 plum tomatoes, peeled, seeded, and chopped

1 carrot, peeled and diced

1 head garlic, halved through its equator

2 teaspoons fresh thyme leaves

1 pound dried white beans, soaked overnight in cold water and drained

6 to 8 legs Duck Confit (page 140 to make your own, or buy from a reputable brand like dartagnan.com)

2 cups coarse fresh bread crumbs (page 268)

Heat the olive oil in a very large, heavy pot over medium-high heat. Add the ribs, sausages, and bacon lardons to the pot and season aggressively with salt and pepper. Cook the meats, turning them occasionally, until browned on all sides, 15 to 20 minutes altogether. A lot of liquid will release from the meats while they're cooking—you want to let them do that and then be patient while the liquid evaporates and they turn a lovely, dark brown. This is where so much of the amazing flavor will come from in the final dish, so hang in there even if it feels like it's taking a while.

Add all of the vegetables to the pot along with the thyme and cook, stirring occasionally, until the vegetables are beginning to soften and the tomatoes have released much of their liquid, about 10 minutes. Add the drained beans to the pot and cover the mixture with water (it will take 3 or 4 cups depending on the depth of your pot). Stir in a large pinch of salt and a few grinds of pepper and bring the mixture to a boil. Lower the heat and simmer, uncovered, until the beans are tender and much of the liquid has evaporated, about 2 hours. While the cassoulet is cooking, be sure to skim off any foam that rises to the surface.

When you're ready to serve, preheat the oven to 400°F.

Place the duck legs on a rack set over a baking sheet and roast in the oven until the meat is warm and the skin crisps, about 20 minutes. Set the duck legs aside.

Meanwhile, top the cassoulet with the bread crumbs, transfer the uncovered pot to the oven, and bake until the bread crumbs are toasted and crisp, about 10 minutes.

Serve the cassoulet in deep bowls, and tuck a crispy duck leg into each portion.

Coq au Vin

Coq au vin, chicken in wine, is a very traditional, casual dish from the countryside of Burgundy. After soaking in wine for at least one night (plan ahead!), the chicken fills with flavor. A traditional *beurre manié* ("kneaded butter"), a mixture of softened butter and flour, thickens the coq au vin and gives it a glossy richness. You can also make a lighter version of this dish using white wine from Burgundy, such as chablis or Pouilly-Fuissé.

A great source for heritage poultry is heritagefoodsusa.com. Using heritage poultry supports the conservation of endangered breeds. These breeds are often a more flavorful and healthy choice for your diet. They also make an exceptional coq au vin due to the fact that they usually live a vigorous and active free-range life.

[SERVES 4]

4 chicken legs and thighs, separated at the joint (8 pieces total)

6 garlic cloves, peeled and crushed

2 cups dry red wine from Burgundy (such as a pinot noir)

One 5-inch stem fresh rosemary

¼ cup extra-virgin olive oil

¼ pound bacon, cut into 1-inch pieces

1 teaspoon Herbes de Provence (page 261)

6 button mushrooms, quartered

1 cup water

1 cup peeled pearl onions (about ½ pound unpeeled)

2 tablespoons unsalted butter, at room temperature

3 tablespoons unbleached all-purpose flour

Coarse salt

Bread, for serving

Remove and discard the skin from the chicken. Grasping the skin with paper towels and pulling it off the meat is the easiest way to do this.

Place the chicken, garlic, red wine, and rosemary in a nonreactive container or pot, or sealable plastic bag that can hold it all comfortably. Cover and refrigerate overnight, or for up to 3 days.

Remove the chicken from the marinade, reserving the marinade, and pat the pieces dry with paper towels. Set the chicken aside. Remove the rosemary and the garlic from the marinade. Discard the rosemary and finely chop the garlic cloves and set them aside. Reserve the wine.

Place the olive oil and the bacon in a large, heavy pot set over medium-high heat. Cook, stirring occasionally, until the bacon begins to crisp, about 5 minutes.

Using a slotted spoon, transfer the bacon to a plate and set it aside. Add the chicken to the pot, working in batches if necessary, and cook until browned on all sides, about 15 minutes total. Return the bacon to the pot, along with the herbes de Provence, mushrooms, reserved garlic, reserved wine, and water. Stir to combine everything. Bring the mixture to a boil, then lower the heat and partially cover with a lid (leave it a bit ajar so that steam can escape). Simmer until the chicken is tender, about 30 minutes. Uncover the pot, add the onions, partially cover the pot once again, and cook until the onions are just tender, about 10 minutes.

Meanwhile, blend the butter and flour together in a small bowl, using your fingers. While whisking, add 1 cup of the cooking liquid to the butter and flour mixture and transfer it to the pot, stirring to combine. Let the mixture cook until the butter and flour mixture has thickened the sauce and given it a slightly glossy, rich-looking appearance, just 5 minutes. Season the coq au vin to taste with salt. Serve alongside your favorite potato recipe, such as Pommes Vigneron (page 186).

Rabbit à la Moutarde

Yes, this recipe works with chicken; but if you haven't ever tried rabbit, I encourage you to seek it out from your local farmers' market or butcher shop. Its mild flavor and tender texture go so beautifully with this simple, creamy mustard sauce, and the entire dish is easy to make. It also reheats beautifully if you'd like to make it ahead. Serve with plenty of good bread to sop up all of the gorgeous sauce.

[SERVES 4]

One 3- to 4-pound rabbit, cut into serving pieces

Coarse salt

4 tablespoons (½ stick) unsalted butter

4 shallots, peeled and finely minced

2 garlic cloves, peeled and finely minced

1 tablespoon Herbes de Provence (page 261)

1 teaspoon dried thyme

1 cup white wine

1 cup heavy cream

¼ cup smooth Dijon mustard

3 tablespoons whole-grain mustard

1 pound small potatoes, boiled until tender and halved

Pat the rabbit pieces dry with paper towels and season aggressively with salt.

Melt the butter in a large, heavy pot over medium-high heat. Add the rabbit pieces and cook, turning only once, until browned, about 5 minutes per side. Transfer the rabbit pieces to a plate and set aside.

Add the shallots and garlic to the pot and cook, stirring occasionally, until just beginning to soften, about 5 minutes. Add the herbes de Provence, thyme, and wine to the pot and bring the mixture to a boil. Whisk in the cream and both of the mustards, then lower the heat and allow the mixture to simmer so that all of the flavors combine, just a minute or two. Season the mixture to taste with salt.

Return the browned rabbit pieces to the pot and simmer, uncovered, until the rabbit is tender, about 20 minutes. Add the cooked potatoes during the last 10 minutes of cooking just to heat them through. Serve hot.

A NOTE ON WINE
Try an admirable French pinot noir from Burgundy, such as Pommard, or Gevrey-Chambertin.

Grilled Oysters
with Shallots

While there is no food more seductive or delicious on its own than a freshly shucked raw oyster, grilling them and anointing them with a simple combination of butter, shallots, and white wine is not to be missed. If you do not have an outdoor grill, shuck the oysters, fill them with the shallot mixture, and then broil them until the juices bubble and the oysters are just cooked through.

[SERVES 4]

4 tablespoons (½ stick) unsalted butter

2 shallots, peeled and finely minced

½ cup white wine

Coarse salt

2 dozen oysters

Melt the butter in a small saucepan over medium heat. Add the shallots and cook, stirring occasionally, until just beginning to soften, about 4 minutes. Add the white wine, increase the heat to high, and allow the mixture to boil and reduce until just barely beginning to thicken, about 3 minutes. Remove the pot from the heat and set aside. Season the mixture to taste with salt.

Meanwhile, place the oysters on a hot grill, flat side up, and cook until the oysters open themselves up, 4 to 5 minutes. Using tongs, carefully, but quickly, transfer the oysters to a tray or a platter. Once the oysters have cooled down enough to handle them, remove and discard the top shells. Be sure not to lose any of the precious juice in the bottom shell (not to mention the oysters!).

Top each oyster with a spoonful of the shallot mixture and return the oysters to the grill, shell side down. Cook until the oysters are hot and their juices and the shallot mixture are bubbling. Serve immediately.

Scallops with Brown Butter and Capers

The combination of nutty browned butter, tart lemon, and salty capers highlights the natural sweetness of scallops. Serve in scallop shells, if you can find them.

[SERVES 4]

1 lemon

A dozen large sea scallops, tough connective muscle detached

Coarse salt

5 tablespoons unsalted butter

2 tablespoons capers, dried on a paper towel

Using a vegetable peeler, remove the zest from the lemon in large strips and cut the lemon in half. Set all aside.

Pat the scallops dry with a paper towel and season them on both sides with salt.

Melt the butter in a large skillet over high heat. Once the butter begins to turn a little bit brown, carefully place the scallops in the pan along with the capers and reserved lemon zest. Cook until the scallops are thoroughly browned on both sides, turning only once, 1 to 2 minutes per side.

Remove the pan from the heat and squeeze over the juice from one half of the reserved lemon. Serve the scallops immediately, being sure to spoon over all of the capers and brown butter.

Grilled Sardines with Salmoriglio

Whether I am grilling seafood, poultry, lamb, or vegetables, I use this southern Italian classic marinade of lemon juice, garlic, oregano, parsley, chilies, and olive oil. This piquant marinade is the perfect complement for char-grilled foods. Keep a bottle full of *salmoriglio* in your refrigerator for up to 5 days. With a good shake, it is ready to go.

[SERVES 4]

Juice of 2 lemons

2 garlic cloves, finely minced or puréed on a Microplane grater

1 teaspoon dried oregano

1 tablespoon finely chopped fresh flat-leaf parsley

¼ teaspoon red chili flakes

1 teaspoon coarse salt

1 tablespoon warm water

A dozen fresh whole sardines, scaled and gutted

A dozen scallions, washed and trimmed

A dozen large escarole leaves (the tender inner leaves can be grilled as well and served alongside, see page 180)

In a small bowl, whisk together the lemon juice, garlic, oregano, parsley, chili flakes, salt, and warm water.

Place the sardines and scallions in a large bowl or baking dish or any vessel that holds them comfortably. Spoon over half of the salmoriglio and set the remaining half aside. Using a spoon or your hands, gently stir the sardines and scallions to make sure that they're fully coated with the salmoriglio and let them marinate for 30 minutes.

Meanwhile, set up a charcoal grill and get it nice and hot, or if you're using a gas grill, set the heat to high. If you're working indoors, set a grill pan over high heat or preheat your broiler to high. Any of these options will work.

Wrap each sardine with an escarole leaf and place them on the grill along with the scallions. Grill everything until charred on all sides and cooked through, 2 to 3 minutes a side for both the sardines and the scallions. Transfer the sardines and scallions to a serving platter and drizzle with the reserved salmoriglio. Serve immediately.

RECIPE NOTE

If you use the salmoriglio beyond sardines, note that chickens should rest overnight in the marinade in the refrigerator, but fish, lamb, and vegetables need just 30 minutes at room temperature. Remember to reserve some of the salmoriglio to drizzle over the food just before indulging.

Brandade de Morue

Brandade de morue is a mixture of whipped salt cod and potatoes and is very satisfying. At Buvette, I serve it in a jar next to a pile of grilled toast. Incidentally, packing it in a jar makes brandade a wonderful picnic snack. Be sure to plan ahead, as the cod must soak for three days.

[SERVES 4]

¼ pound salt cod, skin removed

½ cup whole milk

1 cup heavy cream

3 garlic cloves, peeled

1 large russet potato, peeled and roughly chopped

¼ cup extra-virgin olive oil

Coarse salt

Grilled or toasted bread, for serving

In the refrigerator, soak the salt cod in a big bowl of water for 3 days, changing the water twice daily. Drain and cut the fish into small pieces.

Combine the milk, cream, garlic, and potato in a pot and simmer over medium heat until the potato is just tender, 15 to 20 minutes. Add the chopped salt cod and continue cooking until the fish is tender, about another 15 minutes.

Remove and reserve 1 cup of the cooking liquid, and transfer the remaining mixture to a large bowl. While stirring constantly with a large wooden spoon, add the olive oil in a slow, steady stream. Stir until the mixture is almost smooth, adding a bit of the reserved cooking liquid if necessary. Season the brandade to taste with salt.

Serve warm with plenty of grilled or toasted bread.

> **RECIPE NOTE**
> For a gluten-free alternative, brandade can successfully and deliciously be served on Potato Pancakes (page 184).

Pesce con Patate

Even though it's great looking, the potato crust isn't there just for aesthetics—it envelops the fish, keeping all of its juice and flavor intact. Needless to say, the browned, crispy potatoes are pretty delectable too. If you are averse to cooking a whole fish, feel free to wrap fillets of sea bass with the potatoes and cook as instructed below.

[SERVES 2]

One 1½- to 2-pound sea bass, scaled, gutted, and cleaned (or two 6-ounce fillets)

Coarse salt

Freshly ground black pepper

A few garlic cloves, crushed

2 sprigs fresh rosemary

¼ cup extra-virgin olive oil

2 large Yukon gold potatoes, peeled and thinly sliced on a mandoline

Preheat the oven to 400°F.

Aggressively season both the inside and outside of the fish with salt and pepper. Stuff the cavity with the garlic and rosemary.

Heat the olive oil over medium-high heat in a sauté pan large enough to hold the fish. Add the potato slices to the pan, one at a time, creating a single, blanketlike layer. Season the potatoes with salt and pepper, and place the fish on top of the potatoes. Using a spatula, fold the potatoes over the fish so that it's completely enveloped in the slices.

Transfer the fish to the oven and bake for 10 minutes. Remove the fish from the oven and carefully turn it using two spatulas. Return the fish to the oven and roast until the potatoes are nicely browned and the fish is cooked through, 10 to 15 more minutes. To test for doneness, insert the blade of a paring knife or a metal skewer into the fish and then place it on top of your thumb, on your chin, or on your upper lip—it should be nice and hot, indicating that the heat from the oven has moved its way through the entire fish and it's cooked through.

Lobster Américaine en Croûte

This elaborate dish is very old-fashioned and quite special. It's very "buttoned up" to do this *en croûte* (or under an awning of puff pastry), but you can simplify it and make it a bit more casual by serving the mixture on its own, or back in the empty lobster shells with a stack of toast at your side to mop up all of the lovely sauce.

[SERVES 4]

LOBSTER AND STOCK

Two 1¼-pound lobsters

2 tablespoons extra-virgin olive oil

1 celery stalk, roughly chopped

1 small carrot, peeled and roughly chopped

1 leek, white and light green parts only, well washed and roughly chopped

½ red onion, peeled and roughly chopped

1 small fennel bulb, roughly chopped

4 sprigs fresh thyme

2 fresh bay leaves

½ dozen fresh parsley stems

Coarse salt

2 tablespoons Homemade Tomato Concentrate (page 266), or tomato paste

½ cup white wine

SAUCE AND FINISHING

2 tablespoons extra-virgin olive oil

1 celery stalk, finely diced

1 small carrot, peeled and finely diced

1 small yellow onion, peeled and finely diced

1 shallot, peeled and finely diced

2 tomatoes, stemmed, seeded, and diced

2 garlic cloves, peeled and minced

½ small fennel bulb, trimmed and finely diced

Coarse salt

Pinch cayenne pepper

1 tablespoon Homemade Tomato Concentrate (page 266) or tomato paste

2 tablespoons cognac

½ cup white wine

¼ cup heavy cream

Freshly ground pepper (white pepper is preferable, but totally okay if you only have black)

1 tablespoon fresh tarragon leaves, roughly chopped

1 sheet prepared puff pastry (usually 7 to 9 ounces)

Emotionally speaking, killing the lobsters will likely be the most difficult part of the recipe. But, as with all hard things that are necessary, do it quickly. That said, this is the first step: Working with one lobster at a time, hold the lobster down on a cutting board with a kitchen towel and then confidently place the tip of your chef's knife on top of the lobster's head and swiftly bring the knife down the length of the lobster. I know it sounds like an almost barbaric practice, but to me, and I know many chefs agree, this quick death is the most humane way to kill a lobster. It is much kinder than the slower, labored demise-by-boiling-water. Note that a lobster's nerve endings will sometimes continue to function even after the knife has done its work.

Place the dispatched lobsters into a large baking dish or other vessel that holds them comfortably, pour over enough boiling water to cover them, and let them sit in this very hot bath for exactly 4 minutes. Remove the lobsters from the water and set them aside until they're cool enough to handle. This "blanching" process will not cook the lobster meat all the way through, but it will help to separate it from its shells, making it easier to extract. Note that leaving the lobster partially uncooked at this point compensates for the time it will be in the oven underneath its cap of puff pastry.

Once the lobsters are cool enough to handle, remove all the meat from the shells. Scissors are useful here to cut through the tail, and a swift hit on each of the claws with a mallet or the back of a knife will help to crack the shells, allowing you to pull out the meat. The same goes for the sweet knuckles. Roughly chop the meat into bite-size pieces and set it aside. Reserve all of the shells, being sure to discard the stomach if it's intact.

Meanwhile, to make the stock, heat the olive oil in a large saucepan set over medium-high heat. Add the chopped celery, carrot, leek, onion, fennel, thyme, bay leaves, and parsley stems and cook, stirring occasionally, until the vegetables have begun to soften and brown a bit, about 10 minutes.

Add a large pinch of salt, the reserved lobster shells, and the tomato concentrate (or tomato paste), and cook until the mixture starts to pick up a nice brown, almost rust color from the tomato, 3 to 4 minutes.

Add the white wine, cook for just a minute to burn some of the alcohol off, then pour in enough cold water to nearly cover the mixture. Bring to a boil, reduce the heat, and simmer, skimming off and discarding any foam that accumulates, until the stock has reduced by one-third, about 25 minutes.

Season the stock to taste with salt and then strain through a fine-mesh sieve into a clean pot, bowl, or pitcher and set it aside.

To make the sauce, heat the olive oil in a large skillet set over medium-high heat. Add the celery, carrot, onion, shallot, tomatoes, garlic, and fennel and cook, stirring occasionally, until the vegetables are just beginning to soften, about 5 minutes.

Stir in a large pinch of salt, the cayenne, and the tomato concentrate (or tomato paste) and cook for just a minute or so, or until the tomato just barely begins to take on some color. »CONTINUES

Add the cognac and the white wine and cook over high heat until the liquid has nearly evaporated, 2 to 3 minutes.

Add 2 cups of the reserved lobster stock and the cream, reduce the heat to medium-low, and simmer for just 5 minutes, or until all of the flavors are wonderfully combined. Season the sauce to taste with salt and white pepper.

Stir in the reserved lobster meat and the tarragon and cook for a final minute.

If you choose to skip the "en croûte" portion of the recipe, cook the lobster a little longer until it's just cooked through, about 5 minutes altogether, and then serve it immediately with plenty of toast.

To prepare the lobster en croûte, preheat the oven to 425°F.

Leave the lobster mixture in the pan, place it in a large ovenproof baking dish, or divide it among four individual ovenproof soup tureens. Whichever vessel or vessels you use, brush the outer edge with water (just use your fingertips, unless of course you're keeping the lobster in the hot skillet, in which case use a pastry brush). Drape the puff pastry over the vessel (or cut it into 4 rounds if you're using individual tureens) and press it against the outer edge so it forms a seal. Using a paring knife, poke a small hole in the center of the pastry. If you're using a skillet, place it directly in the oven; if you're using one or more ramekins, place it/them on a sheet pan and place the sheet pan in the oven. Bake until the puff pastry is beautifully browned, about 15 minutes. Serve hot.

Mussels Provençal

Persillade is a paste of garlic, parsley, and olive oil and is a wonderful mixture to have on hand to stir into scrambled eggs, spread onto fish, or toss with roasted potatoes. Mixed with bread crumbs, persillade becomes an indispensable topping for these mussels. If you mix the bread crumbs with plenty of grated Parmigiano-Reggiano, you've got my go-to mixture for stuffing vegetables before roasting them. Try making *petits légumes farcis*, stuffed vegetables, by filling hollowed-out tomatoes, onions, zucchini, or mushrooms.

[SERVES 4]

BREAD CRUMBS

4 garlic cloves, peeled and roughly chopped

1 cup packed fresh flat-leaf parsley leaves, washed and dried

½ cup extra-virgin olive oil

½ teaspoon coarse salt

3 cups ½-inch cubes of day-old bread, crusts removed

MUSSELS

2 tablespoons extra-virgin olive oil, plus more for serving

½ small fennel bulb, trimmed and finely diced

2 shallots, peeled and finely chopped

4 garlic cloves, peeled and finely chopped

2 teaspoons fresh thyme leaves, roughly chopped

Leaves from 2 sprigs fresh flat-leaf parsley, roughly chopped

Pinch red chili flakes

Coarse salt

4 dozen mussels, debearded and scrubbed

1 cup white wine

3 tablespoons pastis

Rouille (page 265), for serving

To make the bread crumb mixture, combine the garlic and the parsley leaves in the bowl of a food processor and pulse until everything is nicely minced. Add the olive oil and the salt and let the machine run until a paste forms, about 1 minute. Add the bread to the machine and pulse until the cubes turn to crumbs and the entire mixture is saturated with a vibrant green color and has the texture of wet sand, about ten 10-second pulses. Set the mixture aside. »CONTINUES

To prepare the mussels, heat the olive oil in a large pot over high heat. Add the fennel, shallots, garlic, thyme, parsley, and chili flakes and cook, stirring occasionally, until just beginning to soften, 2 to 3 minutes. Season the vegetables liberally with salt. Stir in the mussels to combine them with the aromatics. Pour the wine and pastis over the mussels and bring the mixture to a boil. Reduce the heat to medium, cover the pot, and cook until all of the mussels have opened, about 5 minutes. Remove the mussels from the heat. Discard any mussels that have not opened.

At this point, you can portion the mussels into four large individual bowls, or onto one large serving platter. Scatter the crumbs over the mussels, pour over the broth, and serve immediately.

Alternatively, you can wait until the mussels are cool enough to handle and then individually stuff each one with about a tablespoon of the bread crumb mixture and line them up in a skillet or on a sheet pan and broil them until the bread crumbs go a bit crunchy.

Place the broiled mussels into four large bowls or onto one large serving platter and pour the cooking liquid (which you've kept hot, mind you) over the top.

Whether or not you take the step to broil them is up to you, they are good both ways. Either way, be sure to serve them alongside a bowl of Rouille, which you can spoon onto your mussels as you eat them—pretty much heaven as far as I am concerned.

PART 7.

SWEETS

Sweets

I've been working off educated guesses for a long time—in and out of the kitchen. This is especially true when it comes to making desserts. I've rarely worked in restaurants large enough to have a pastry chef so, even though I'm untrained, I've often been my own dessert department.

I've developed a small repertoire of classic desserts that satisfy both my sweet tooth and my love for working with my hands. Beating egg whites for Mousse au Chocolat (page 234), using just a big bowl and a whisk, or peeling a case of apples for Tarte Tatin (page 243) are fulfilling tasks that I've come to look forward to. But for the days when I don't have time to make something so labor-intensive, I've come to rely on a handful of remarkably simple desserts that everyone seems to love. And remember, a bowl of ripe seasonal fruit and a spoonful of Nutella is sometimes all you need.

Flourless Chocolate Cake

I had my first flourless chocolate cake in the Marais, in Paris, while I was in college (not) studying history. The slice of cake was served to me unadorned, with a fork stuck in it. If I failed to mention my suburban upbringing, sponsored by Sara Lee and Betty Crocker, let me confirm it here now. Needless to say, I was quite impressed with the cake, and Paris too. This recipe has been in my repertoire for more than twenty-five years and it hasn't changed.

[SERVES 8]

12 tablespoons (1½ sticks) unsalted butter, cubed, plus more for the pan

¾ pound (12 ounces) semisweet chocolate, roughly chopped

6 large eggs, separated

1½ cups sugar

Pinch coarse salt

Preheat the oven to 325°F. Generously butter a 9-inch springform pan and set it aside.

Put the butter and chocolate in a bowl set over a small pot of barely simmering water. Stir until completely melted. Set the chocolate mixture aside to cool slightly.

Meanwhile, put the egg whites in a large mixing bowl, or into the bowl of a stand mixer fitted with the wire whip, and whip until they form soft peaks. Add ¾ cup of the sugar to the egg whites and continue whisking until they're shiny and stiff peaks are just beginning to hold. Set the egg whites aside.

In a separate bowl, whisk the remaining ¾ cup sugar with the egg yolks until the mixture is thickened and pale yellow. Whisk in a healthy pinch of salt.

Whisk the chocolate mixture into the egg yolks, one-third at a time, making sure each addition is completely combined before adding the next. Don't be tempted to add the chocolate all at once—adding it in batches will help regulate the temperature of the egg yolks and keep them smooth and uniform. Carefully fold the beaten egg whites into the chocolate mixture, being as gentle and careful as possible so as not to lose any of the volume you have worked so hard to create in the egg whites.

Pour the batter into the prepared pan and bake until it's just barely firm to the touch and a paring knife comes out clean when you pierce the cake, about 20 minutes. Remove the cake from the oven and allow it to cool for at least 20 minutes before slicing and serving. Note that although the cake will almost inflate and swell with air as it bakes, it will collapse and crack when it cools down. This is a good thing—beautiful, even. And serving with crème fraîche never hurts!

RECIPE NOTE

If you'd like, sprinkle this cake with chopped, candied almonds halfway through the baking time for a crunchy, sweet layer.

Chocolat Chaud

I have enjoyed hot chocolate while standing in Bar San Calistro, a dive bar in Rome, where it's served in little water glasses with unsweetened cream, and I've had it at Angelina on the Rue de Rivoli in Paris served in monogrammed porcelain cups set on silver trays in a room with frescoed walls. Both are capable of breaking my heart. After roasted chestnuts, hot chocolate topped with whipped cream is one of my favorite parts of winter. At Buvette, bowls of hot chocolate are an after-school tradition, along with chocolate-stained faces.

[SERVES 4]

½ cup heavy cream

4 cups whole milk

1 tablespoon cornstarch

¾ pound (12 ounces) semisweet chocolate, roughly chopped

Pinch coarse salt

Pour the cream into a large mixing bowl and whisk until it forms soft peaks. Alternatively, you can do this with an electric mixer, but be careful not to overwhip the cream. Set the whipped cream aside.

In a small bowl, whisk ¼ cup of the cold milk with the cornstarch and set the mixture aside.

Place the remaining 3¾ cups milk in a large saucepan over low heat and warm until bubbles just begin to appear around the edge. Do not let the milk boil!

Add the chocolate and the salt to the warm milk and whisk until the chocolate has completely melted and the mixture is smooth. Whisk in the reserved cornstarch mixture; this will give the chocolate a velvety texture.

Pour the hot chocolate into mugs and top each serving with a quarter of the whipped cream.

> RECIPE NOTE
> The hot chocolate can be easily reheated over a double boiler, so feel free to make it up to a week ahead and keep it, covered, in the refrigerator.

Mousse au Chocolat

Less is often more. Case in point: we offer two desserts at Buvette—this chocolate mousse and Tarte Tatin (page 243). But sometimes less is really more, as most customers can't decide and order both! Try giving new use to old things by serving the mousse in demitasse cups, or by the spoonful topped with crème Chantilly (lightly sweetened whipped cream).

[SERVES 4 TO 6]

12 tablespoons (1½ sticks) unsalted butter, cut into small pieces

½ pound (8 ounces) semisweet chocolate, roughly chopped

1 tablespoon water

3 large eggs, separated, plus an additional egg white

Pinch coarse salt

2 teaspoons superfine sugar

Crème fraîche or lightly sweetened whipped cream, for serving

Put the butter and chocolate in a stainless-steel bowl along with the spoonful of water and set over a small pot of barely simmering water. Stir until completely melted. Set the chocolate mixture aside to cool slightly.

Whisk the 3 egg yolks together in a large mixing bowl with the salt. Set aside.

Meanwhile, place the 4 egg whites in a large mixing bowl, or into the bowl of a stand mixer fitted with the wire whip. Add the sugar and beat until stiff peaks form.

Whisk the yolks, one-third at a time, into the chocolate mixture, making sure each addition is completely combined before adding the next. Don't be tempted to add the egg yolks all at once—adding it in batches will help regulate the temperature of the egg yolks and keep them smooth and uniform.

Next carefully fold the stiff egg whites into the chocolate mixture, being as gentle and careful as possible so as not to lose any of the volume you have worked so hard to create in the egg whites. Cover the bowl with plastic wrap and set in the refrigerator until firm, at least 4 hours and up to 2 days in advance.

Scoop the mousse, which will have become a striking combination of fluffy and dense, into serving bowls and serve with crème fraîche or lightly sweetened whipped cream.

On Securing Your Bowl
When you are whisking anything vigorously (egg whites, for example, or even mayonnaise), it's helpful to have your bowl nice and secure. My favorite way to do this is to twist a barely damp kitchen towel into a circle underneath the bowl and, voilà, the bowl rests securely in the towel, allowing you to whip and whisk with abandon.

Chocolate and Grappa Truffles

Made of grape stems, grappa has the same variety of flavors you find in wine, and combining it with chocolate is a great way to temper the "firewater" quality it can sometimes have.

[MAKES ABOUT 2 DOZEN TRUFFLES]

½ pound (8 ounces) semisweet chocolate, chopped

½ cup heavy cream

2 tablespoons grappa

Pinch coarse salt

High-quality cocoa powder, for rolling

Put the chocolate into a large mixing bowl and set aside.

Stir together the cream, grappa, and salt in a saucepan over medium-high heat. When the cream mixture begins to form bubbles around the edges, but before it comes to a full boil, remove the pot from the heat. Immediately pour the cream mixture over the chocolate and let it sit for 2 minutes to allow the heat to melt the chocolate. Vigorously whisk everything together or, if you have one, blend the mixture together with a handheld immersion blender. Either way, you want the chocolate and cream to be completely emulsified. Let the chocolate cool to room temperature (you can speed this up by pouring it into a baking dish or something else with more surface area), then refrigerate it until it's firm, at least 2 hours. At this point, the chocolate mixture can sit in the refrigerator, covered, for up to a week.

Once the chocolate is solid, place a pile of cocoa on a large plate. Drag a warm spoon across the chocolate to make curls. Don't worry about making them perfect. Actually, avoid making them perfect. They should be irregular and varied. Place the curls in the cocoa and toss them to coat. Transfer the finished truffles to a serving platter or into a container. While they keep well, covered, in the refrigerator for a week or so, it's best to eat them at room temperature.

Almond Toffee

Almond toffee is a great recipe for beginning candy makers. Serve it with an espresso as a café gourmand, the assortment of sweets that come with coffee in the late afternoon in Paris. It also makes a great gift.

[MAKES 1 POUND CANDY]

16 tablespoons (2 sticks) unsalted butter, plus extra for the pan

2 cups roasted almonds

1 cup sugar

1 teaspoon coarse salt

½ cup semisweet chocolate chips (3.5 ounces)

Generously butter a half sheet pan and set it aside.

Coarsely chop 1 cup of the almonds and set them aside. Finely chop the remaining 1 cup almonds and set them aside separately.

Transfer the coarsely chopped almonds to a heavy saucepan along with the butter, sugar, and salt. Set the pan over high heat and cook, stirring occasionally, until the mixture has become a golden brown caramel and registers 300°F on a candy thermometer, 5 to 6 minutes.

Carefully pour the caramel onto the prepared sheet pan and allow it to spread naturally. Evenly distribute the chocolate chips over the top of the caramel while it is still hot. Once they melt from the heat of the caramel, sprinkle the chocolate layer with the reserved finely chopped almonds. Allow the toffee to cool and then break it into pieces. Store in a covered container in the refrigerator. Serve at room temperature.

> **How to Clean a Sticky Pot**
>
> *If you are left with a sticky pot with sugar stuck on it, whether from Almond Toffee, Orange and Campari Marmalade (page 40), or Tarte Tatin (page 243), simply return the pot to the stovetop and boil water in it until the caramelized sugar dissolves and the pot is left clean.*

Chocolate-Dipped Figs and Gooseberries

These were some of the first things I ate when I went to Italy, and their beautiful simplicity was part of what made me fall so deeply in love with Italian food and culture. To make these, simply melt chopped semisweet chocolate in a bowl set over a small pot of barely simmering water. Peel back the papery skin from the gooseberries (the small orange fruits also sometimes called ground cherries)—be sure to leave the papery skin attached. Holding the stem, dip the berries into the chocolate and transfer them to a baking sheet lined with a cooling rack or parchment paper to set. You can speed this up by placing the dipped fruits in the refrigerator. Repeat with the dried figs. You can make this with any fresh or dried fruit, and feel free to stuff the dried fruits with nuts. Figs and walnuts are terrific together, as are apricots and almonds.

Madeleines

When the madeleines are ready at Buvette, a little chalkboard appears in the window advertising them. They are dusted with powdered sugar and kept warm between folded napkins on small white plates and are usually served with tea.

[MAKES A DOZEN MADELEINES (OR 3 DOZEN MINIATURE ONES)]

4 tablespoons (½ stick) unsalted butter, plus more for pan

½ vanilla pod and its seeds, scraped out (or substitute 2 teaspoons pure vanilla extract)

2 large eggs

⅓ cup sugar

½ cup unbleached all-purpose flour, sifted, plus more for pan

Pinch coarse salt

Zest of ½ lemon

Powdered sugar, for serving

Combine the butter, the scraped vanilla pod, and the vanilla seeds in a small skillet and set it over medium-high heat. (If you're using vanilla extract instead of the vanilla pod, add the vanilla extract later as instructed.) Cook the butter until it froths, then gets quiet and turns a dark brown color and smells wonderfully nutty, about 3 minutes. Be sure to keep an eye on the butter as it's cooking, so that it doesn't burn and turn black. Once it's browned, set it aside to cool and then remove and discard the vanilla pod, if you used one.

Meanwhile, put the eggs and sugar in the bowl of a stand mixer fitted with the whisk attachment and beat on high speed until the mixture thickens significantly and turns pale in color. Alternatively, you could use an electric handheld mixer or just a whisk and a lot of elbow grease.

Thoroughly whisk the flour and the salt into the egg mixture. Whisk in the lemon zest and the reserved browned butter, being sure to get all the vanilla seeds into the mixture. If you're using vanilla extract instead, now's the time to add it. Scrape down the sides of the bowl with a plastic spatula to make sure there are no pockets of flour or egg hiding anywhere.

Transfer the batter to a container, or simply cover the bowl with plastic wrap and let it chill in the refrigerator for at least 2 hours and up to 2 days before baking. Resting the batter will help the madeleines puff up in the oven and ultimately have a wonderfully light texture.

Once the batter has chilled, preheat the oven to 350°F. Generously butter and flour a madeleine tray (even if it's nonstick). Divide the batter evenly among the molds, filling each one three-quarters of the way up. Tap the tray on the countertop to deflate any air bubbles, then transfer the tray to the oven.

On Vanilla

I am skeptical of any processed ingredient, even vanilla extract. I prefer scraping the seeds from a whole vanilla bean and then saving the pod to infuse brown butter or flavor a canister of sugar.

On Flouring Your Pan

When you are flouring any pan, especially a madeleine pan with all of its small and particular crevices, a small shaker fitted with a wire mesh top filled with flour is your best friend. You can find these at any kitchen or restaurant supply store (note that they are normally sold as "sugar shakers"). With one of these in hand, a controlled, even layer of flour becomes an easy achievement rather than a big mess.

Bake the madeleines until they are just firm to the touch and ever so lightly golden brown, about 12 minutes. While still warm, remove the madeleines from the tray (tapping its edge firmly on your kitchen countertop makes easy work of this), and dust them generously with powdered sugar. Serve them warm, in a basket lined with a napkin.

Tarte Tatin

Sometimes I see beautiful *galettes* in the windows of bakeries with pains-takingly thin slices of perfect apples, all arranged in concentric circles, the whole thing a pale shade of gold. Just gorgeous. And all I can think is *why would you have that when you could have a tarte Tatin?*

[SERVES 6 TO 8]

½ cup sugar

9 apples (see Recipe Note page 244), peeled, halved, and cored

1 sheet prepared puff pastry (usually 7 to 9 ounces)

Crème fraîche, for serving

Caramel Glaze (optional) (see page 244)

Preheat the oven to 425°F. Line a baking sheet with aluminum foil.

Pour the sugar into a heavy, ovenproof 8-inch skillet and place over medium heat. Give the pan one quick shake so that the sugar is in an even layer. Let the heat and the sugar do the work. It needs no stirring or swirling until the sugar caramelizes, about 8 minutes. Do not walk away while the caramel is forming because it can burn very quickly! When the caramel is dark amber in color, immediately turn off the burner and remove the skillet from the heat. If you do not have a heavy, 8-inch skillet, you can make the caramel in a small pot and then pour it in an even layer into an 8- or 10-inch cake pan and go from there.

Once the caramel has cooled down a bit (it doesn't have to be room temperature, but you don't want it to be boiling hot), arrange the apples in the skillet by placing each one on its side and snugly tucking each consecutive one as closely together as possible to form tight, concentric circles. Really pack in the apples and pile any extras on top. It will seem like too many, but they will shrink as they cook and release a lot of liquid.

Cover the apples tightly with aluminum foil, being sure to seal the edges. This will hold in the steam, which will help the apples to cook evenly and thoroughly. Place the skillet on the foil-covered baking sheet (to catch any juice that might come out) and bake in the oven until the apples are wonderfully soft and collapsed, about 1 hour.

Remove the skillet from the oven and discard the foil. Rearrange the apples, if necessary, as some may have shrunk. (See Caramel Glaze directions on the next page.) Set the pan over high heat and cook until the juices are completely reduced and sticky and, when you shake the pan, all of the apples start to move as a single layer, just 3 or 4 minutes. Be careful not to burn the apples and the caramel. Once the juices have reduced, remove the skillet from the heat and carefully »CONTINUES place the puff pastry over the apples, trimming it so it fits the skillet. Place the skillet back on the baking sheet, return it to the oven, and bake until the puff pastry is really nicely browned, 35 to 45 minutes.

Remove the tart from the oven and let it rest for 10 minutes. Place a large plate over the puff pastry and *very carefully* invert the tart, being very cautious not to burn yourself (caramel is hot, dangerous stuff). Let the skillet sit, upside down, over the plate for a minute or two so that gravity begins to do its job, and the apples release from the bottom of the pan. Without shaking the pan, slowly lift it up and away as the tart remains on the plate. If a few of the apples stick to the pan, simply help them out with a spoon—no big deal and no one will know!

Cut the tarte Tatin into slices and serve hot, or at room temperature, with plenty of crème fraîche and caramel glaze (see below), if you like.

CARAMEL GLAZE

If you don't mind an extra step and a small pot to wash, you can easily make a shiny, thick glaze to cover the tarte Tatin. When you take the apples out of the oven after they've cooked, instead of reducing the liquid on the stovetop, carefully pour the liquid off into a small saucepan, being sure not to disrupt your apple arrangement. The easiest way to do this is to cover the pan with a pot lid and tip the pan into the saucepan so that the lid catches any apples that threaten to escape. Cover the drained apples with the pastry and tuck it into the oven as instructed. Meanwhile, boil the strained liquid until it is dark golden brown and quite thick and set it aside. Once you've inverted your tarte Tatin, use a spoon to evenly cover the apples with the glaze.

> RECIPE NOTE
> **On Choosing the Right Fruit**
> I use Gala apples for tarte Tatin, but you can use other types if you'd like, including Golden Delicious or Honeycrisp. Be sure, no matter which type you use, that your apples are all the same size so that they cook evenly.

Roasted Applesauce

Steal the caramelized apples from the tarte Tatin to make an exceptional applesauce, especially good for topping Potato Pancakes (page 184). To make it, once the apples are done baking, but before they are topped with puff pastry, mash them with a fork, season to taste with salt, and eat hot, at room temperature, or cold.

Peaches Roasted in Amaretto

Amaretto is a sweet Italian liqueur made from apricot and almond pits, which has a round, nutty flavor. Pouring it over ripe summer peaches and sending the combination into the broiler to caramelize yields a delicious and memorable dessert that could not be easier to make. As with all simple things, the results depend entirely on the quality of your ingredients so only make this when you have great peaches on hand.

[SERVES 4]

4 peaches

¼ cup amaretto

½ cup sugar

Crème fraîche or Fior di Latte Gelato
(page 250), for serving

Preheat the broiler to high.

Halve the peaches and remove and discard the pits.

Place the peach halves in a skillet that will hold them in a single layer. Pour the amaretto over the peaches and sprinkle with the sugar. Place the skillet on the stovetop over high heat to burn off the alcohol, about 3 minutes. Pay attention when the amaretto cooks off its alcohol, taking care not to burn the mixture. Transfer the pan to the broiler and broil until the peaches are browned and the liquid has reduced to a honeylike consistency, 5 to 10 minutes. Serve the peaches hot, warm, at room temperature, or even cold. These are just perfect by themselves or with a bit of crème fraîche or Fior di Latte Gelato.

Digestifs

A glass of cognac, Calvados, or Armagnac is very nice following a meal. Known as **digestifs,** *the liquors contribute to what I consider the art of the digestif, which is the ritual following dinner that marries gastronomy and conviviality, and aids digestion. I like to drop off a tray of cognac and glasses at the table and let my guests help themselves. Arcane etiquette: digestifs are always passed to the left and poured by oneself.*

Roasted Pears

Bosc pears are better suited for roasting than Bartletts or Fiorellos. They can be enjoyed warm or cold on their own as a winter dessert, or served alongside a wedge of blue cheese.

[SERVES 4]

4 medium Bosc pears

2 cups red wine

½ cup sugar

1 cinnamon stick, if you have one

Preheat the oven to 400°F.

Place the whole pears, *au naturel,* in a small ovenproof skillet standing upright side by side. Pour the red wine over the pears and sprinkle with sugar. Add the cinnamon stick and bake for 45 minutes, until fork-tender and a sweet glaze has formed. More wine or water may be added if the liquid is reducing too fast.

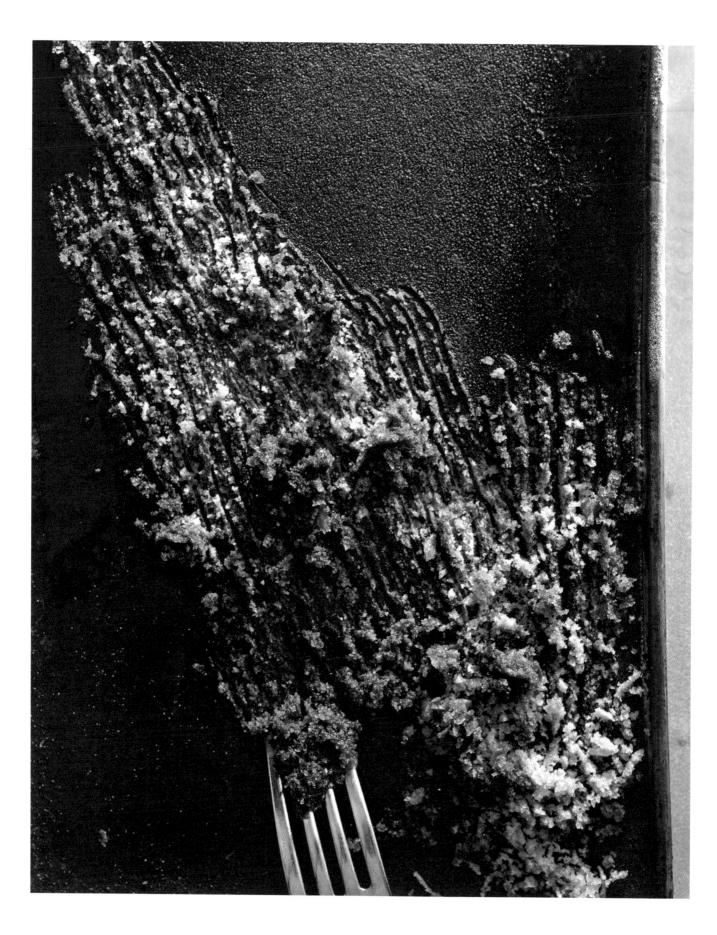

Espresso Granita

In Rome, *granita* and *grattachecca* (shaved ice with syrups) are a summer tradition served from colorful kiosks, with perpetual lines, along the Tevere. This espresso granita must be completely frozen before serving, so plan ahead and note that it can be kept, covered, in the freezer for up to a month.

[SERVES 4]

2 cups very strong cold-brewed coffee or espresso

½ cup light brown sugar

½ cup heavy cream

Pour the coffee or espresso into a small saucepan and stir in the sugar. Set over medium heat and cook, stirring, until the sugar has completely dissolved, 2 or 3 minutes.

Let the coffee cool to room temperature then pour it into a shallow metal pan and freeze until solid, about 3 hours. Place six glasses into the freezer as well.

Meanwhile, pour the cream into a large bowl and whip with a wire whisk until it forms soft peaks. Set the cream aside.

Using a fork, scrape the frozen coffee to form icy shavings, and scoop the shavings into the cold glasses. Top each serving with some of the whipped cream and serve immediately.

Fior di Latte Gelato

Fior di latte roughly translates to "milk blossoms," and the clean, sweet flavor is the pinnacle of ice cream purity. All it needs are some fresh strawberries as an accompaniment.

[MAKES 1 QUART GELATO]

2 cups whole milk
2 cups sugar
Pinch coarse salt
2 cups heavy cream

Combine the milk, sugar, and salt in a saucepan over low heat and cook just until the sugar has completely dissolved, being careful not to scorch the milk. Now would be the time to infuse the gelato to your heart's desire if you were going in that direction (perhaps a sprig of rosemary, a handful of coffee beans, or crushed green cardamom pods), then strain out the flavorings.

For our simple purposes, we will just remove the sweetened milk from the stovetop, pour it into a bowl, and stir in the cold cream to cool down the milk. Cover the mixture and refrigerate it until it's very cold, at least 1 hour.

Transfer the mixture to your ice cream maker and churn according to the manufacturer's instructions. Or get some friends together to churn the gelato the old-fashioned way with a vintage, hand-cranked White Mountain ice cream maker.

Scoop the gelato directly from the freezer and serve immediately.

RECIPE NOTE

If you do not have an ice cream maker (neither a contemporary one nor an old-fashioned one), you can make gelato in sealable plastic bags. Fill one large bag with 6 cups of ice, 2 cups of kosher salt, and 1 cup of water; the combination creates a below-freezing temperature. Place the chilled gelato mixture into another bag and zip it closed. Place the gelato bag into the bag of icy salt and zip it shut. There should be enough icy salt mixture to completely submerge the gelato bag, and it is vital that both bags be zipped, so consider double-bagging each. Once you're set up, shake the bags vigorously until the gelato thickens, 15 to 20 minutes. While this doesn't make gelato as thick as a machine would, and it requires a lot of cold shaking, it is fun and a great way to keep children entertained.

Some Very Simple Desserts
to Entertain With...

There's an Italian saying, "*a tavola non si invecchia,*" which translates to "at the table you never get old." For those planned gatherings or impromptu moments, here are five of my favorite ways to capture time and enjoy life bite by bite.

I. Include a silver tray with digestifs like Calvados and Fernet-Branca and cordial glasses. Let it sit on the table, tempting your guests to consider just one more. Encourage them to help themselves (after all, they will know just how much to pour).

2. Can anyone pass up just a spoonful of something sweet? Even after dessert, a tray of spoons filled with chocolate mousse (page 234) or even Nutella is a lovely gesture as a thank-you.

3. All my favorite meals finish with seasonal fresh fruit. It could be cherries on ice, a basket of grapes, or slices of watermelon for your family or guests to share. When preparing a bowl of ice for fruit, place a clean cloth napkin folded under the ice. This way as the ice melts the napkin absorbs the water. Consider things like cherry pits and grape stems, and always provide plates for discarding them.

4. Ordinary things can be made elegant, like a bowl of fresh raspberries spiked with Moscato or Pineau served on special china or even in demitasse cups.

5. In the evenings at Buvette we set out leather baskets of walnuts, almonds, and hazelnuts for the guests to help themselves. On special occasions I bring out vintage nutcrackers. We may add roasted chestnuts, blocks of *torrone*, and dried fruit dipped in chocolate (page 238) to end the meal too.

Sweets   253

PART 8

THE LARDER

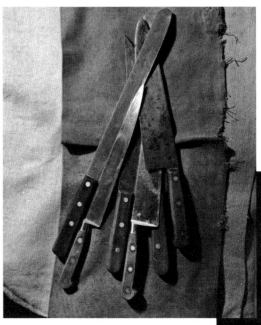

The Larder

Preparing meals becomes an easy, doable routine when things like olive oil, crème fraîche, mustard, vinegar, mayonnaise, capers, and butter are in reach. Cooking becomes even more interesting when you go from merely keeping your pantry stocked to building a larder.

Traditionally, larders were cool areas in homes, typically cold cellars, which were used for food storage before refrigerators became commonplace. Nowadays, a larder has become more a personal tradition of canning, pickling, and other do-it-yourself crafts, and suggests being resourceful and economic. A larder is also about pre-paredness, having tins of anchovies and jars of jam on your shelf, a stack of clean kitchen towels folded nearby, and knowing how to keep copper polished. Having a larder means honoring the age-old traditions of keeping a home running, and taking pleasure in the time these tasks require.

A larder is also very much about give and take. It's about accepting jars of homemade jam from a neighbor and remembering to put them out when you have the neighbor over for breakfast. It's about drying bundles of herbs and crushing them for herbes de Provence and storing them in jars to use in your cooking and also to offer as a housewarming gift. Keeping a larder means being able to easily make a pot of soup for a friend who is ill, or making more vinaigrette than you need, knowing that your dinner guest might want to take some home so that they are one step closer to mak-ing dinner for their family. The following pages include my favorite larder recipes and many tricks of my trade. Pass them on.

Crème Fraîche

I would not touch a piece of Tarte Tatin (page 243) without crème fraîche. One of my most frequently used ingredients, crème fraîche is in many of my recipes. If you can't find it, here's how to make it. Plan ahead if you want to make this from scratch, as it will take some time.

[MAKES 2 CUPS CRÈME FRAÎCHE]

2 cups heavy cream
2 tablespoons buttermilk

It is as easy as mixing the heavy cream together with the buttermilk. Let the mixture rest, unrefrigerated, at 70°F for 10 hours, or until thickened. Stir, cover, and refrigerate. The crème fraîche keeps well in the refrigerator for up to 10 days.

Vinaigrette

This is a classic vinaigrette for dressing salads as well as chilled vegetables or legumes. It is, by far, my favorite vinaigrette for its flexibility and reliability.

[MAKES 1 CUP VINAIGRETTE]

2 large shallots, peeled and very finely diced
1 teaspoon fresh thyme, finely chopped
1 small garlic clove, finely grated on a Microplane grater
3 tablespoons sherry vinegar
½ cup extra-virgin olive oil
1 tablespoon water
Pinch sugar
½ teaspoon coarse salt
A few grinds freshly ground black pepper

Whisk all of the ingredients together until they're well combined. Store in the refrigerator for up to a month.

> **RECIPE NOTE**
> You can easily turn this into a mustard vinaigrette by whisking in 2 tablespoons of smooth Dijon or whole-grain mustard.

Basil Pesto

In the middle of summer, when basil is growing waist high, I start making batch upon batch of basil pesto. I remember fondly standing over the sink at Caffé Arti in Italy, cleaning bags of basil, and the entire room would smell green and sweet. Instead of a mortar and pestle, we used a meat grinder and randomly dropped in chunks of Parmigiano-Reggiano cheese with handfuls of toasted pine nuts together with basil leaves and olive oil. The final product was a perfect pesto, drenched in olive oil, coarse and verdant.

[MAKES 2¼ CUPS PESTO]

2 packed cups fresh basil leaves
(about 3.5 ounces)

¼ pound Parmigiano-Reggiano cheese, roughly chopped or coarsely grated (about 1 cup grated)

¼ cup pine nuts, lightly toasted

1 garlic clove, peeled and roughly chopped

1½ teaspoons coarse salt

1 cup extra-virgin olive oil

Whether you are using a meat grinder, mortar and pestle, or food processor the technique is similar. Combine the basil, cheese, pine nuts, garlic, and salt, and grind together. Slowly drizzle in the olive oil. The pesto should have a nice coarse texture. Topped with olive oil and stored in an airtight container, the pesto will last for a week or two in the fridge.

RECIPE NOTE

Cleaning Basil and Other Leafy Herbs

To wash basil, fill a large bowl or a clean sink with cold water and tumble in the basil leaves. Agitate them in the water so that any dirt clinging to them falls to the bottom of the water. Gently lift the leaves out, leaving the sand on the bottom, draining the water and making sure any dirt goes with it. Fill the bowl or sink once again with clean cold water, and repeat the process. If the basil is especially dirty, do it a third and final time. Run the leaves through a salad spinner and then lay them out on paper towels to dry. This method works with any leafy herbs and all lettuces.

Herbes de Provence

I use this traditional French mix of dried herbs from Provence in so much of my cooking. While you can buy it in jars at the store, I like to make my own in order to take advantage of the abundance of fresh herbs during the summer. I simply hang them in a dry corner of the kitchen and then, once they're nice and dry, I pull the herbs off their stems, crush them, and put them in a jar that I keep by my stove where they soon find their way on top of Croque-Monsieurs (page 69), into pots of Coq au Vin (page 206), into Ratatouille (page 179), and more. Herbes de Provence brighten all grilled and roasted meats, fish, and vegetable dishes. Any leftovers from a chicken that has been rubbed with olive oil and herbes de Provence and roasted makes the best chicken salad in the world. Simply shred it, skin and all, and mix it with a good amount of Mayonnaise (page 264).

[MAKES AS MUCH AS YOU LIKE]

I use equal parts of the following
in my mixture:

Dried savory

Dried thyme

Dried rosemary

Dried lavender

Dried basil

Dried marjoram

Dried sage

Fennel seeds

Mix the herbs together and store in a sealed jar in a cool, dark place.

Pâté Spice

This fragrant combination of spices is essential for both duck rillettes (page 140) and Pâté de Campagne (page 147). Even if you don't make either of those dishes often, the spice mixture can be stirred into hot milk with honey for a variation on Staff Masala Chai (page 61), or incorporated into roast meats, cake batters, or anything else that would welcome the warming flavors.

[MAKES 2 TABLESPOONS SPICE MIX;
EASILY MULTIPLIED]

1 teaspoon ground cloves

1 teaspoon freshly grated nutmeg

1 teaspoon dried ginger

1 teaspoon ground coriander

2 teaspoons ground cinnamon

Stir everything together and store in a sealed jar in a cool, dark place.

Buvette / The Pleasure of Good Food

Pickles

Keep in mind pickling liquids and brines should be well balanced with salt, vinegar, and sugar. In a word, they should be drinkable, and tasting the mixture should be enjoyable. This pickling mix strikes a nice chord and can be used for whatever vegetables you like.

[MAKES 2 QUARTS PICKLES]

1 cup white vinegar

3 cups warm water

3 garlic cloves, peeled

2 tablespoons coarse salt

1 tablespoon sugar

2 green cardamom pods

2 fresh bay leaves

1 dried arbol chili

1 teaspoon coriander seeds

2 sprigs fresh thyme

4 cups vegetables (root and cruciferous vegetables will need to be blanched before pickling)

Combine all of the ingredients except for the vegetables in a saucepan over high heat and bring to a boil. Reduce the heat and simmer until the sugar and salt have dissolved. Taste for seasoning and adjust as needed. Divide the vegetables between two 2-quart containers and pour the liquid mixture evenly over until the vegetables are completely submerged. Close the containers and refrigerate at least overnight before eating. The pickles will last in the refrigerator for up to a month.

Pickled Horseradish

This easy-to-prepare, bracing condiment is wonderful to have in your larder. Serve it alongside any slowly cooked meat that needs a little assertive accompaniment. It can be stirred into crème fraîche for a quick, punchy sauce that livens up roasted beets (page 172) or makes a wonderful sauce for Potato Pancakes (page 184), especially when served with smoked salmon. Whisked into Mayonnaise (page 264), this pickled horseradish makes an incredible spread for a roast beef sandwich.

To make pickled horseradish, peel a fresh horseradish root, grate it, and place it in a jar. Pour in sherry vinegar until it comes halfway up the horseradish and then pour in enough water to cover the horseradish. Stir to combine and place a lid on the jar. Store it in the refrigerator for up to a month. Both the horseradish and the pickling liquid are wonderful condiments that can be used as one, or separately.

Mayonnaise

Making mayonnaise by hand for the first time is like stepping into a brightly lit space without realizing you've been in the dark. You see how the simplest ingredients can become an elegant sum of their parts. Growing up in California, we often made a dinner out of mayonnaise and Steamed Artichokes (page 98). At home, I make a quick mayonnaise using a fork and a plate instead of a whisk and a bowl, mainly because then it's really easy to clean up!

[MAKES ½ CUP MAYONNAISE; EASILY MULTIPLIED]

1 large egg yolk

A squeeze of fresh lemon juice (about 1 teaspoon)

1 teaspoon water

Pinch coarse salt

6 or 7 tablespoons extra-virgin olive oil

Whisk together the egg, lemon, water, and salt and then very, very slowly, whisk in the olive oil, just a few drops at a time at first, building up to a slow, steady stream. The mixture should be the color of mustard and thick enough to hold itself together. This is luscious, precious stuff. Serve immediately or place in an airtight container and refrigerate for no more than 2 days.

RECIPE NOTES

Aioli

Make the mayonnaise recipe and add a teaspoon of Dijon mustard and a bit of finely grated garlic (if there is a green sprout in the middle of your garlic clove, remove and discard it as it is bitter). Uses for aioli range from fresh vegetables like asparagus to fried sardines.

Sauce Gribiche

Make the mayonnaise recipe above and add 1 roughly chopped hard-boiled egg, 1 teaspoon of Dijon mustard, 1 tablespoon roughly chopped capers, 6 chopped cornichons, extra salt and pepper, and the leaves from 2 stems of tarragon, roughly chopped. Serve with poached salmon, cooked and thinly sliced tongue, cold roasted or poached chicken, or on a fried skate sandwich (see Recipe Note page 75).

Rouille

Rouille is a bread-thickened mayonnaise originally from Provence in the south of France. It is traditionally served with *bouillabaisse*, the wonderful seafood stew from the area. I use it alongside Mussels Provençal (page 225). It's also really good for sandwiches or dabbed onto hard-boiled eggs. Feel free to add saffron to the rouille if you'd like by simply adding a pinch along with the chili flakes.

[MAKES 1 CUP ROUILLE]

1 slice (about 1 ounce) day-old bread, cut into ½-inch cubes (about 1 cup cubes)

1 roasted red bell pepper, skin, seeds, and stems removed and discarded, roughly chopped

1 small garlic clove, roughly chopped

Pinch red chili flakes or cayenne pepper

1 egg yolk

½ cup extra-virgin olive oil

Juice of half a lemon

½ teaspoon coarse salt

Combine the bread, roasted pepper, garlic, and chili flakes into the bowl of a food processor and pulse until the mixture is uniformly minced. Alternatively, you can make the rouille in a blender or using a mortar and pestle.

Add the egg yolk to the bread mixture and process until fully incorporated. With the machine running, slowly pour in the olive oil in a steady stream. Add the lemon juice and salt and let the machine run until the rouille is wonderfully smooth and creamy, about 1 full minute. Taste for seasoning, and add more salt or lemon if you think it needs it. Serve immediately or store in an airtight container in the refrigerator for up to 1 week.

Clarified Butter

I use clarified butter to create a seal over the crocks of Chicken Liver Mousse (page 142) and Salmon Rillettes (page 144). It is also great for cooking since it can withstand higher temperatures than butter because you've removed the milk solids, which are what burn so easily. Try it for cooking potatoes or fish.

[MAKES SLIGHTLY LESS THAN ½ CUP CLARIFIED BUTTER]

8 tablespoons (1 stick) unsalted butter, cut into pieces

Slowly melt the butter in a saucepan over low heat. Once the butter has completely melted, a few minutes, remove the pot from the heat and let it sit for 5 minutes. Skim off and discard the foam that will have risen to the surface, and slowly pour the clarified butter into a container, leaving the milky solids in the bottom of the pot. Discard the solids. The clarified butter keeps, covered, in the refrigerator for a month.

Homemade Tomato Concentrate

This highly concentrated paste of sun-dried tomatoes can be used anywhere you would use canned tomato paste. It's great for soups and sauces. It's also an essential ingredient in the grand Lobster Américaine en Croûte (page 220). Note that if the sun-dried tomatoes are very dry and salty, soak them in warm water first until they have softened, then drain them and proceed with the recipe.

[MAKES 2 CUPS CONCENTRATE]

1 pound sun-dried tomatoes, roughly chopped

3 garlic cloves, crushed

1 cup extra-virgin olive oil, plus extra for storing

Put half the tomatoes and garlic in the bowl of a mortar and pestle and work into a smooth paste with a drizzle of the olive oil. Repeat with the other half. Pack the mixture into a clean container and pour a thin layer of olive oil over the top; this will help keep oxygen out. Stored in the refrigerator, the concentrate will keep for a couple of months. Just be sure to replace the oil each time you use a spoonful.

> **RECIPE NOTE**
> You may also use a food processor to make the concentrate. Simply pulse the tomatoes and garlic with the olive oil into a smooth paste.

Tomato Confit

When faced with a surplus of tomatoes in the summer, try this technique of peeling and seeding them, then very slowly drying them out in a low oven. The result is almost like a sun-dried tomato. Use them to top schiacciata (page 70), or add them to salads.

[MAKES ABOUT 2 CUPS CONFIT]

A dozen vine-ripened tomatoes

½ cup extra-virgin olive oil, plus a little bit more

Preheat the oven to 250°F.

Bring a large pot of water to a boil.

Meanwhile, using a sharp paring knife, score the bottom of each tomato with a shallow X. Carefully place the tomatoes into the hot water and let them cook until their skins start to loosen, about half a minute, maybe a whole minute at the most. Using a slotted spoon, remove them from the water and set aside until they're cool enough to handle.

Once the tomatoes have cooled down, peel off and discard the skins and cut each tomato crosswise in half. Using a teaspoon, scoop out and discard the seeds from each tomato half.

Place the tomatoes in a baking dish that holds them comfortably in an even layer. Pour over the olive oil and bake in the oven until they're quite dry and concentrated, about 6 hours. Transfer the tomatoes to a jar and cover with a thin layer of olive oil. Cover the jar and store the tomatoes in the refrigerator where they will keep for a couple of weeks.

Seasoned Salts

Use a ratio of 3 parts salt to 1 part spice or herbs. Coarsely grind together the salt and your favorite spices in a mortar with a pestle, or in a food processor. I often use a combination of fennel seeds and black pepper in the fall and switch to coriander and cumin seeds in the summer. No refrigeration necessary. Use to season meats, fish, and eggs.

Old Bread

Leftover bread still has promise in it. A day-old chunk of bread is perfect to soak in water and vinegar for the Heirloom Tomato Salad with Cucumbers and Bread (page 84). Leftover bread or fresh bread can be made into bread crumbs, which are essential to many of my favorite recipes, including Mussels Provençal (page 225), Meatballs (page 194), and Cassoulet (page 204). To make bread crumbs, remove the crust, tear the bread into small pieces, and pulse in a food processor to fine crumbs. Now the bread crumbs are ready for toasting or soaking, depending on the recipe. Bread crumbs don't keep well, so it is best to make them as needed.

Béchamel

This makes a very dense béchamel, perfect for spreading on bread for "croques" (page 69), or for using in a mixture for a croquette. If you need a thinner, looser béchamel, such as for a cheese sauce, simply add more milk.

[MAKES ¼ CUP]

1½ tablespoons unsalted butter

2 tablespoons unbleached all-purpose flour

½ teaspoon freshly grated nutmeg

¾ cup whole milk

Coarse salt

Combine the butter, flour, and nutmeg in a heavy saucepan over medium heat. Cook, stirring with a wooden spoon, until barely browned, 3 to 4 minutes. Gradually stir in the milk and cook, stirring constantly until the mixture thickens and begins to pull away from the edges of the pan, 3 to 4 minutes; you are looking for a mixture that has the consistency of a thick pudding. It will stick to the spoon and should have some elasticity. Remove the béchamel from the heat and season to taste with salt.

Tomato Sauce

This utterly simple tomato sauce is essential for Meatballs (page 194) and is also good to have on hand for simple pastas or to poach eggs in. I never made tomato sauce once during my three years in Reggio Emilia since it's not part of the northern Italian repertoire. But when I got to Rome, the bucatini changed everything!

[MAKES 2 CUPS SAUCE]

¼ cup extra-virgin olive oil

1 sprig fresh basil

3 garlic cloves, peeled and finely chopped

One 28-ounce can crushed tomatoes, preferably San Marzano

1½ teaspoons coarse salt

Pinch red chili flakes

Place the olive oil in a large saucepan over low heat. Add the basil and garlic and cook until just golden, about 5 minutes. Add the tomatoes and their juices along with the salt and chili flakes. Let the sauce simmer over low heat until thick, about 45 minutes. Remove and discard the basil sprig before serving.

> RECIPE NOTE
> This sauce must be cooled before being refrigerated and can be kept, refrigerated, for up to 2 weeks.

Healthy Household Cleaning Tips

CUTTING BOARDS

To deodorize and brighten wooden boards, cut a lemon in half and work it into the board with a handful of salt. Lemons and salt are a natural bleach and antiseptic.

STOVETOPS

Cooking and cleaning go hand in hand. Knowing that grease will remove grease will save you some time when the cooking is done. Rub out stubborn grease spatters with an oiled cloth. For more shine use a paste of baking soda and water for a nonabrasive cleaner.

COPPER POTS

As an apprentice I did my share of grunt work. In Kurashiki, Japan, I was responsible for washing and folding the kitchen towels at the end of each dinner service. In Reggio Emilia, Italy, I polished the copper pots among other things. To clean copper, make a paste out of equal parts lemon juice (or white vinegar), flour, and salt. Simply rub it all over your copper and rinse off the paste. Dry with a cotton towel and watch them shine immediately—works like a charm!

SILVER

I am an avid collector of old silver trays, cake stands, candy dishes, and teapots. I find mixing and matching different pieces delightful. To give your silver pieces a little sparkle, soak them in a nonreactive container lined with a small sheet of aluminum foil and filled with ¼ cup ammonia, 10 cups warm water, and a capful of soap. Rinse and dry the silver with a cotton towel.

KITCHEN FIRST AID: ALOE VERA

It's wise to keep an aloe vera plant in or near your kitchen for its soothing and healing properties. In the event you cut or burn yourself, neither pleasant but both inevitable, cut a piece of aloe and place the cut side directly on your wound.

A Self-Taught Cook

Jody Williams's hands become animated when she talks about a dish. She chops the air, flips something in a nonexistent sauté pan, pretends a piece of paper is a crêpe and explains how to fold it. One day while we were working on this book, she got so carried away telling me about Aligot (page 185), pretending to stretch the elastic potatoes, that she abandoned a baking sheet of beets she had been roasting! "Ooh, bad Jody!" she says, aloud, to herself, taking them out of the oven. "What's the matter?" I asked her. "They don't look like they enjoyed their time in there." She splashes the baking sheet with a bit of water and tucks a piece of aluminum foil over the top and folds it around the edges as if putting a fitted sheet on a bed. She puts the baking sheet back in the oven, sighs loudly, and says, "Your intention really does count for everything."

Jody's intention, as it were, is quite simple: she wants all the puzzle pieces to fit. With dishes influenced by both history and her personal travels, her food is informed both by collective memories and her own nostalgia too. Her cooking is simple and seasonal, and she expresses unmitigated respect for her ingredients and the setting her dishes are served in. At Buvette, her perfect slip of a restaurant tucked on a charming stretch of Grove Street in New York City's Greenwich Village, Jody has fully realized her puzzle.

Buvette is the kind of place you can go to every day (and many do). Its doors open at 8:00 a.m. every weekday morning, 10:00 a.m. on the weekends, and don't close until 2:00 a.m. It feels so good to be inside Buvette that you can't help but leave a little happier than you arrived—in other words, it's a total escape. It's a place where you can press pause, where you can leave your phone in your pocket, where work seems just a little less urgent.

Jody accomplishes this all through her intrinsic sensibility that steers her toward everything good. Her menus are full of classic dishes, refreshingly *not* re-invented. They're also full of simple plates featuring great ingredients that she's not afraid to leave alone. Cheese, for example, is looked after and always served

at the right temperature, while a leg of prosciutto is perpetually poised on its Berkel slicer, ready to be cut at any moment. While she has a full liquor license, she only lists three cocktails on her menu: a Manhattan, a Martini, and an Old-Fashioned. Presenting her customers with an edited selection guarantees that there's no such thing as a bad choice. Buvette runs, it seems, on a terrific mix of restraint and generosity.

Jody's good taste applies not only to Buvette's menu, but also to the entire atmosphere. The place is flush with good lighting and beautiful surfaces, the long bar a cool slab of marble. There's good glassware and plenty of ice in the lemonade and nothing moves to or from a table unless it's on a silver tray. Baskets of apples and lemons sit in front of the bathrooms where gorgeous soap and fragrant, but not too fragrant, lotion is installed by the sink. Every moment you experience has been considered and curated.

Translating the experience of eating and drinking at Buvette to the page required Jody to dig deep, to recollect all the stories, people, trips, lessons, even the failures and bumps in the road that got her to where she is today—all the puzzle pieces, so to speak. This entire book is filled with all of the dishes that accompany these memories.

Recently I was with Jody going through some of her old ephemera. She's got everything stored here and there, mostly cigar boxes bursting at the seam with menus from every restaurant she's cooked in (with notes scribbled on them, mostly of phone numbers for local takeout places!), letters from chef friends, grocery lists and food cost breakdowns scribbled on the backs of napkins, photographs from her time in Italy, portraits of her grandmother holding a hunting rifle and a fishing rod. Pointing to it all, taking in this lifetime of travel and work, she sighed. "This is what it looks like," she said, "when you've taught yourself how to cook."

—*Julia Turshen*

Acknowledgments

This book is a collection of many joyous meals I've shared in France and Italy and re-create daily with the help of a great number of dedicated and wonderful people. I would like to extend a heartfelt thanks to my talented cooks, tireless servers, growers, food artisans, vintners, and of course my lovely guests who make Buvette such a unique and pleasurable place. I also wish to thank the many people who so effortlessly captured and shaped the spirit of Buvette for this book.

Let me start with a warm thanks to my writer, the affable and accomplished Julia Turshen, whose skill with words coupled with her intuition and innate curiosity about all things food and drink made her an awesome accomplice. With intelligence and humor, Julia guided this book from a pile of kitchen notes and hours of rambling dialogue to the final pages. She tested each and every recipe without compromising its simplicity or flavor.

I am in debt to the collaborative efforts of the award-winning photographers Andrea Gentl and Martin Hyers, whose artistic and impeccable sensibilities gave beauty to this book. They curated each shot with care using their handmade backdrops and unearthed props. I was humbled to see how easily they could elevate a simple ingredient with light and shadow into an artful subject. Thank you to the entire photography team who worked long and hard to produce the amazing images day after day. Meredith Munn, Alpha Smoot, Jennifer Koehl, Kalen Kaminski, Chaunte Vaughn, Paola Ambrosi de Magistris, and Rob Magnotta.

Special thanks to the gracious Anna Kovel, who styled and sourced the beautiful ingredients. She set the bar high with her knowledge, talent, and impeccable taste; her enthusiasm and expertise were indispensable.

I owe much gratitude to all my cooks at Buvette who contributed their talents to these pages: Erika Kirch, Yoko Ueno, Malika Lieper, Lorena Galicia, Sam Kirk, and my chef de cuisine, Jose Luna. Thank you to Caryne Hayes, our general manager, who always greeted the challenges of making a book with consummate professionalism and hospitality. I am lucky to have the participation and designs of the talented Maximiliano Poglia, who created the handsome wood-block image and graphic designs for Buvette. And to my Paris team Thomas Gardez, Claudia Bellini, and Linda Eglin Mayer, a merci beaucoup à vous for sharing your passions for this project.

Years ago, Janis Donnaud, my agent, began turning the wheels of this project, which brings me to a special thanks to Karen Murgolo, my editor, and her team at Grand Central Life & Style: Kallie Shimek, Pippa White, Anne Twomey, Sonya Safro, and Tom Whatley. Thank you to book designer Gary Tooth as well.

When we needed more room to cook and shoot, our neighbor and my partner, Rita Sodi, lent us her kitchen and dining room at her restaurant, I Sodi. Thank you for the endless support and all the free lunches. I couldn't ask for a more supportive person to partner with on all scales.

I wish to thank a few of our dear suppliers for their hard work and great taste: Anne Saxelby of Saxelby Cheesemongers, Patrick Martins of Heritage Foods, beekeeper Claire at Catskill Provisions, Jenny & François, Royal Crown Bakery, forager Evan Strusinski, and Kermit Lynch Wine Merchant.

And finally, to Mario Batali for always finding the joy in life and for his endless encouragement, and to Alice Waters for her support and leading by example.

Thank you all.

Index

Note: Page numbers in *italics* include photos of dishes.

About the Author

JODY WILLIAMS is chef and owner of Buvette, a gastrothèque she opened in 2010, which has been voted one of New York's Top 10 Restaurants by *Travel & Leisure* and "New York City's Best Breakfast" by Zagat's. Williams's cooking has been praised in such publications as *Bon Appétit, Martha Stewart Living, Travel & Leisure, Gourmet, Glamour, Elle, The New Yorker, The Wall Street Journal, The New York Times, New York* magazine, *Time Out New York*, French *Elle*, and Grub Street. Williams trained with Thomas Keller at Rakel and Lidia Bastianich at Felidia, in addition to working in some of the best kitchens in Italy and France; and she has headed up kitchens at notable restaurants in New York City.

Williams recently opened a second Buvette in Paris. She lives in New York City and Paris.

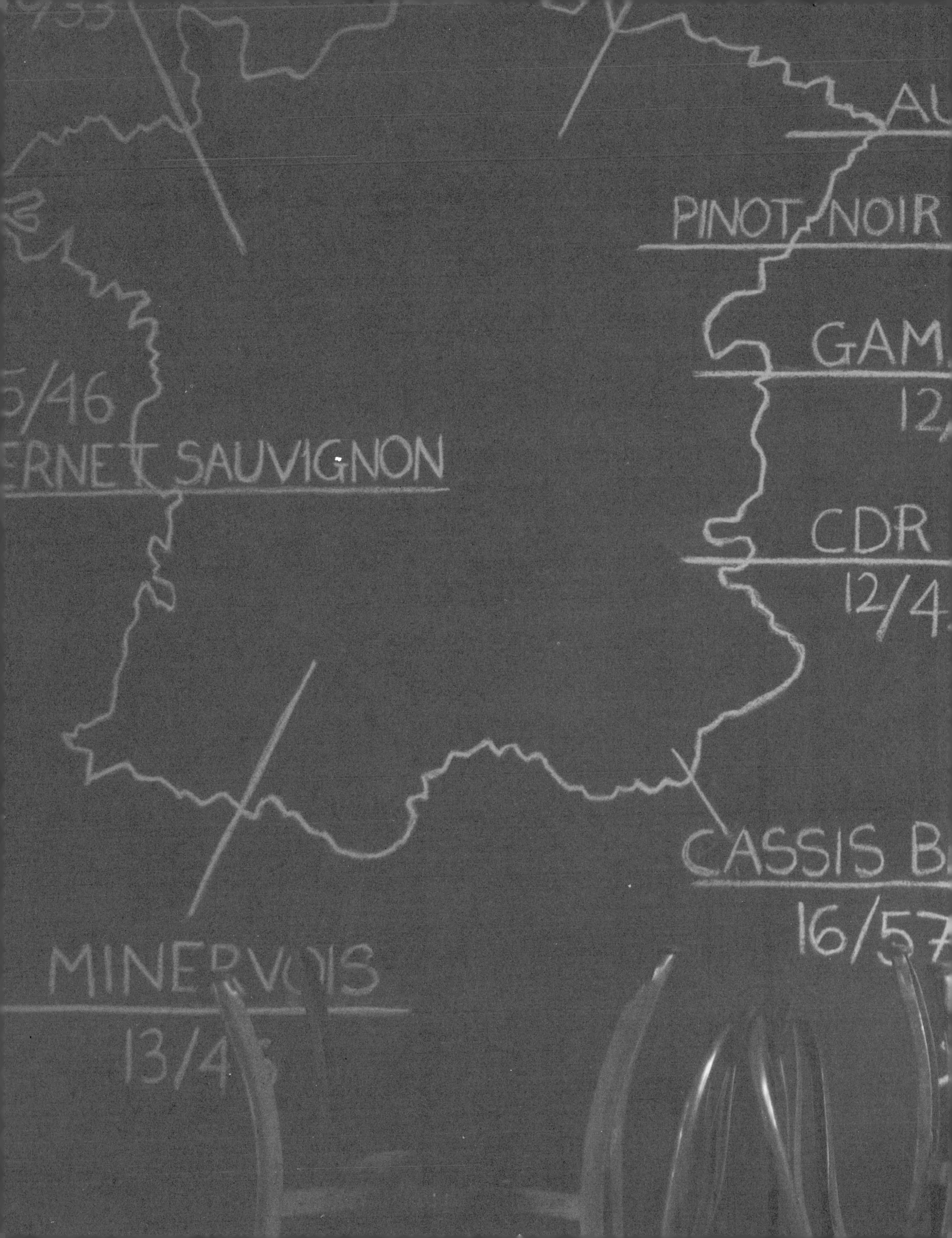

933

PINOT NOIR

GAM.
12

5/46
ERNET SAUVIGNON

CDR
12/4

CASSIS B
16/57

MINERVOIS
13/4